D0857831

HACKING DIGITAL LEARNING STRATEGIES

HACKING DIGITAL LEARNING STRATEGIES

10 Ways to Launch EdTech Missions in Your Classroom

Shelly Sanchez Terrell

PUBLICATIONS

Hacking Digital Learning Strategies
© 2017 by Times 10 Publications

These books are available at special discounts when purchased in quantity for use as premiums, promotions, fundraising, and educational use. For inquiries and details, contact us at www.hacklearning.org.

Published by Times 10
Cleveland, OH
HackLearning.org

Project Management by Rebecca Morris
Cover Design by Tracey Henterly
Interior Design by Steven Plummer
Editing by Jennifer Jas
Proofreading by Nicole Francoeur

Library of Congress Control Number: 2017945360
ISBN: 978-0-9985705-6-3
First Printing: September, 2017

CONTENTS

MISSION TOOLKIT

INTRODUCTION

Mission-based learning to inspire students

I REMEMBER WALKING INTO my college computer lab full of internet-connected computers in 1996. To ace my microcomputer class, I had to learn HTML and create my own GeoCities website. It was full of silly animations and information, but back then my viewers couldn't interact with my website. They couldn't even leave comments. I was excited just to design a website with content for others to view.

Since its inception, the internet has transformed greatly for our students. It is now participatory and engaging and packed with possibilities. Technology has empowered our students, who realize they have the potential to learn anything in exciting ways from incredible institutions and fascinating people. Most of our students want to connect with people around the world, share their passions and creations with an audience, and exchange knowledge. In fact, many are already sharing their passions.

One example is Robby Novak, best known for portraying Kid President and encouraging millions on YouTube and other social media channels to be awesome and kind. Kid President began making a presence when he was just eight years old. At age thirteen, he now travels around the world as a motivational speaker and raises awareness for various movements.

I would like to imagine my students like Kid President, inspiring others with their online activities. The reality is that many students do scary things on social media. They bully, spread false news, share too much with strangers, post inappropriate images of themselves, and make other bad choices. Social media is such a huge part of kids' lives, development, and upbringing, that we can no longer naively stand by while they navigate the digital world alone. It's time to guide them to make more meaningful choices with their use of technology and social media.

To aid you in this great endeavor, this book outlines ten missions (chapters) to inspire students to reflect on their responsibilities as citizens navigating a digital and physical world. Each mission challenges students to use technology to make a meaningful impact and introduces them to the concept of mission-minded learning. We can encourage students to tap into their potential to accomplish great things in the world with their digital behavior.

We send astronauts, explorers, superheroes, military heroes, church leaders, and agents on missions to improve people's lives with their skills and knowledge. We give them background information and tools to accomplish their missions, and they realize the missions are tied to meaningful purposes. In the same way, we should tie school lessons and activities to meaningful purposes that go beyond making good grades or passing tests. This book provides you with the right language, motivation, and resources to send your students on meaningful digital learning missions. Feel free to accomplish the missions in any order. You'll discover a host of tips and guidelines to adapt the tasks to meet your students' needs even if you have limited resources.

We divided each mission into sections similar to other books in the *Hack Learning Series*; however, we titled the sections differently to fit the language of mission-based learning. We replaced the typical *Hack Learning Series* sections – The Problem, The Hack, What You Can Do Tomorrow, A Blueprint for Full Implementation, Overcoming Pushback, and The Hack in Action – with related sections titled The Problem, The Mission, Mission Prep, Mission Launch, Overcoming Mission Obstacles, and The Mission in Action.

The Mission Toolkit, located at the end of the book, is packed with templates, handouts, web tools, apps, and resources to print or download. It also includes Mission Cards (Kit 26) that list each mission with a quick explanation of objectives. You can print the cards and distribute them to students as a physical representation of their missions. And finally, the Mission Toolkit includes Digital Badges (Kit 27) that you may want to share with your students at the completion of each mission, much like the patches that Girl Scouts and Boy Scouts earn. Read more about the idea behind digital badges in Mission 9.

Mission-minded learning is critical for our students, who already play important roles as they navigate the internet. Students can be citizen scientists who share field research and contribute to the collective knowledge of the world. They can act as citizen journalists who share images, videos, audio, and updates about current events in real time. And they can act as activists who support social movements and try to reform policies and laws.

The internet has redefined the way we research, communicate, write and publish books, fundraise, market ideas, and start enterprises. The ten missions in this book introduce teachers and students to the digital skills they need to thrive and succeed as future professionals, authors, creators, innovators, subject matter experts, entrepreneurs, fundraisers, and leaders. These missions will inspire students to reflect on their responsibilities as digital citizens, to connect learning with a meaningful purpose, and to tap into their potential to accomplish great things with their digital behavior.

MISSION 1

DESIGN A GAME WALKTHROUGH

Create a Tutorial and Teach Others How to Play

*It is the supreme art of the teacher to awaken
joy in creative expression and knowledge.*
— ALBERT EINSTEIN, THEORETICAL PHYSICIST

THE PROBLEM: TEACHERS DO TOO MUCH TEACHING

AFTER MY FIRST year of teaching English as a Second Language (ESL) classes in high school, I was asked to teach an unfamiliar subject, World Religions. The previous teacher had suddenly left. There was no curriculum, only a textbook. Our ESL program consisted of seventy-five students from more than ten countries, and I knew my students had way more experience and expertise about world religions than I did.

I made the decision to let the students do most of the teaching. I grouped students and let them choose a religion to present, and directed them to create a hands-on learning activity for the class. My students exceeded my expectations. They dressed in customary attire, played music, and showed artifacts. We practiced dances, learned songs, and participated in rituals. Everyone learned so much, including me!

This experience taught me a valuable lesson. I don't have to do all the teaching or know all the answers. Often, learning is more powerful when students take the reins. Unfortunately, most classroom instruction focuses way too much on the teacher sharing expertise, versus the students. Traditional curriculums rarely allow room for students to design instructional content and walk others through the process of achieving a task or gaining knowledge. The majority of curriculums still treat students as consumers of information. When students lack motivation or are not engaged, it may be because they feel their knowledge and ideas are not valued.

THE MISSION: TEACH OTHERS HOW TO PLAY A GAME WITH A VIDEO WALKTHROUGH

Students hunger to share their knowledge. Many even produce their own video tutorials and how-to videos and post them online as a hobby. Video game walkthroughs are among the most popular forms of video tutorials created by young people. In a traditional walkthrough, gamers share tips and strategies for completing a section of a game, including screenshots. Gamers also record themselves playing a game and share strategies and tips through live audio commentary. They may post these video walkthroughs on YouTube.

For this mission, your students will create a video tutorial about one of their favorite activities – playing games. Your students will take on the role of the teacher and demonstrate strategies for playing a section of a video game. Not only does this provide students with the opportunity to plan instruction for their peers, but they gain experience using a screen-recording tool to highlight important strategies in their videos.

At the end of this mission, you will have a rich collection of student-produced videos, which offer different learning paths for future students to explore.

Producing a video walkthrough develops students' reading and writing skills with digital media. Students learn how to write simple, clear, and concise instructions, which align with the video visuals and action. Furthermore, they complete a storyboard, a strategy that professionals use to produce video content. Most important, this mission shows students they can help a wide variety of people by producing effective video tutorials – an invaluable life skill.

MISSION PREP

The gaming community considers many of the video walkthroughs posted on the internet as "playthroughs." These videos often show inexperienced players fumbling through the game, and viewers don't learn much. We want our students to actually teach peers to complete game tasks.

- **Write down instructions to complete a simple task.**
  I still remember when one of my teachers had us
  give her instructions to make a peanut butter and
  jelly sandwich. She had the ingredients on the table.
  When I told her to put the jelly on the bread, she
  put the jar of jelly on the bag of bread, which made
  the class laugh. This example taught us how to give
  detailed instructions. Conduct a similar lesson where
  students write down instructions to complete a
  simple task, like wrapping a gift or making a paper
  airplane. Display the instructions on a projector or
  read them aloud while following the instructions
  precisely. With each step, get the class to decide on
  the best way to word that instruction. Then host a
  class discussion about writing clear instructions.

- **Use a walkthrough to play a game.** Introduce students to an online learning game they haven't played.
  Students play the first section of the game without
  using a walkthrough. Then they use a video or
  written walkthrough to guide them as they play the
  game again. Encourage students to compare these
  game-playing experiences with their peers. Teacher
  Kyle Mawer provides a great list of learning games
  with walkthroughs at Kylemawer.wikispaces.com.
  Also, find walkthroughs at Visualwalkthroughs.com,
  Strategywiki.org and Jayisgames.com. These websites

only provide written walkthroughs. To find video walkthroughs, search YouTube for the name of the game followed by the word "walkthrough."

- **Analyze exemplars.** Show students two or more examples of video walkthroughs for the same game, and take a vote on their favorites. Invite them to share what they liked or didn't like about each example, and use these ideas to come up with the criteria for designing their video walkthroughs.

MISSION LAUNCH

Step 1: Choose a game for the video walkthroughs.

Computer-based sandbox games are the easiest to manage for this mission. These types of games, like Minecraft, allow students to roam freely in a virtual world and create their own fun with a choice of tools. They are learning opportunities, too. For example, while students are directing their characters to build structures, they are learning chemistry or math skills in the process. While students are planning and constructing towns or cities, they are contextualizing their learning. With these capabilities, students can align their walkthrough tasks with learning objectives from your curriculum.

Step 2: Create a storyboard to plan the video production.

Filmmakers plan out their video productions with storyboards. A storyboard is a graphic organizer that illustrates a sequence of scenes, followed by the dialogue and filming directions.

Storyboarding strengthens your students' writing and video productions by providing a framework for planning and revising. In the Mission Toolkit at the end of this book, you'll find a storyboard template for a game walkthrough (see Kit 1). It works well when students complete the storyboard while playing the game. This way they know the pace of the game action and understand the amount of time they have to provide clear and straight-to-the-point instructions. They can also note any angles or effects they would like to capture or highlight in their videos.

Step 3: Gather feedback on the written instructions.

Students invite their peers to play the game following the written instructions in the storyboard, and to provide constructive criticism. Peers will evaluate whether the storyboard is simple to follow, whether the sequence of the instructions makes sense, and whether the grammar is on-point – providing another excellent learning opportunity (no one wants to read poorly written instructions). Students will then edit the steps according to their peers' feedback.

Step 4: Record and produce the walkthrough with a screencasting tool.

Demonstrate the screencasting tool they will use to produce their walkthroughs. Consider free tools such as Screencast-o-matic and Screencastify. Students will want to explore the tool's features, and practice zooming in and out of scenes, playing with the highlight and spotlight tools, and adding transitions, effects, and captions. In my experience, students enjoy learning about these design elements and deciding how to best use these features to improve their instructional videos – skills that professional designers and producers use daily. Give students time to produce and edit their video walkthroughs. Encourage them to use the storyboards they created in Step 2 to frame their shots and guide their live video commentary. Also, provide instructions for submitting their videos.

Step 5: Watch the video walkthroughs to complete game tasks.

To be meaningful missions, the walkthroughs need to work! Assign students to try to complete tasks in the games using the strategies shared in their peers' walkthroughs. We can assign this as meaningful homework, as many of our digital learners are used to playing games at home. Allocate at least a few days for students to accomplish the tasks. When finished, this is another opportunity for additional feedback. Encourage students to explain any difficulties they encountered and to give recommendations for improvement.

Step 6: Publish the video walkthroughs.

This learning mission shows students how they can use digital tools to help a wide variety of people. At the end of this mission, you will have a rich collection of student-produced videos, which offer different learning paths for future students to explore. Encourage others to watch these video walkthroughs by adding them to a video channel, such as YouTube, SchoolTube, or Vimeo.

OVERCOMING MISSION OBSTACLES

Kids may not realize the higher-order skills that this mission demands, since they are teaching others how to play a video game. Additionally, parents and school leadership may express concerns about students learning via online games. Here are a few more obstacles you may encounter, and how to face them.

Why is my child wasting time playing a video game? Many parents do not see the learning value in playing games. To create buy-in, introduce parents to the game and point to good examples of teachers using the game to support student learning. The Minecraft Education website has lesson plans and examples by teachers in every subject. Learners can replicate many of these activities in other learning games. Also, show parents the activities you designed to ensure students achieve the curriculum objectives. In addition to learning the content in an engaging and interactive way, students achieve these objectives:

- Produce clear and concise instructions.

- Strengthen writing skills by storyboarding, revising, and editing.

- Use technology to design instructional content and share their expertise.

- Use a web tool to record, edit, and produce a video tutorial.

Should kids be laughing and conversational in the videos? Playing games often leads to expressions of enthusiasm and enjoyment, and this means learning is fun. This is totally appropriate for an audience of gamers and young people. Let it slide unless your learners act inappropriately or offensively. At the same time, we want to make sure students understand the importance of delivering good, simple, concise, and understandable strategies. The activities in the Mission Prep will help students outline criteria for a good video walkthrough. Many people learn how to use products or accomplish tasks using online video tutorials. Badly produced and poorly designed instructional content wastes people's time, and in some cases could be dangerous. Emphasize responsibility to students alongside the permission to have fun.

What if students' instructions aren't clear? Many learners make the mistake of crafting instructions based only on their experiences. We need to teach students how to consider their audience when creating their video walkthroughs. Guide them to imagine a peer playing the game for the first time, and encourage them to create instructions with this person in mind. Help students determine what the audience needs to know to accomplish the tasks in the game, including the game's terminology. Students need to introduce the characters, tools, or accessories, and explain why their choices of each are beneficial for the section of the game they are playing.

THE MISSION IN ACTION

When I taught in Croatia, I met the nine-year-old son of my teacher friend, Marijana Smolcec. Filip's advanced grasp of English and his speaking skills astonished me! He was eloquent and spoke English with confidence. When I asked him how he learned English, he said that he and his younger brother watched video tutorials on YouTube. Then he introduced me to his own YouTube channel, MrSnake, and described himself as a professional gamer who loved playing Minecraft. While I watched, he played his video walkthroughs, which showed him accomplishing different tasks on Minecraft. He recounted how he began playing Minecraft at a young age and wanted to be the best, so he watched and learned from other video walkthroughs. He loved the walkthroughs so much that he decided to create his own YouTube channel.

The videos I saw were well made with captions, effects, and music. I had no problems viewing the graphics or following along with Filip's movements or actions. His instructions were easy to understand, although he often laughed or shouted "Wow!" while playing the games.

Filip explained how producing these video walkthroughs motivated him to improve his English and to beef up his technical skills. Though his channel was already impressive, he told me all about his plans to improve the quality and add even more effects. Hearing about his experience introduced me to a whole world of young learners sharing their knowledge and learning from each other. Some students even made a little money when advertisers paid them for ad space on the instructional videos.

When students need to learn how to do something, they often YouTube it. Students know they will find a video tutorial to demonstrate how to accomplish just about anything, and it's inspiring to discover tutorials created by young people just like them. So many of our learners already produce videos to share their expertise with the world. Students need to learn how to deliver simple and clear instructions and produce videos that illustrate these instructions. In this mission, students share their expertise with peers based on something they enjoy doing: playing video games.

Meaningful learning occurs when we provide students with opportunities to share their expertise and help others achieve success. They are more invested in their learning when they feel their teachers value their knowledge and allow them to take the lead. Perhaps most important is that this mission gives kids a sense of achievement and a desire to do even more in the future.

MISSION 2

GO ON A SELFIE ADVENTURE
Define Yourself Through Images

Taking pictures is savoring life intensely,
every hundredth of a second.
– MARC RIBOUD, FRENCH PHOTOGRAPHER / PHOTOJOURNALIST

THE PROBLEM: STUDENTS IGNORE THEIR DIGITAL IDENTITIES

THE SELFIE – a picture of oneself – has become a cultural phenomenon with the evolution of mobile devices and their built-in cameras. Our students often take selfies and share them with peers through messaging apps or on social media. Taking selfies is an important part of a student's sense of self, self-belief, and self-esteem. When students post selfies, they realize that their peers will perceive and rate them. Peers may like the image and perhaps leave positive or negative comments. Students realize that certain pictures receive more positive feedback than others. This experience prompts them to take several selfies and evaluate which ones their peers will like best – an important reflective process that young learners may not fully comprehend.

  Inspire students to reflect on the narratives their selfies present and to live the next chapter of their lives more meaningfully.

The selfie does not necessarily depict how kids see themselves in reality. Instead, selfies are an altered sense of self. Students might change angles, distort their bodies, or add filters and edit their selfies to portray themselves as skinnier, taller, sexier, funnier, or more mysterious. In essence, they manipulate the selfie to display characteristics and personality traits that they may or may not possess. Additionally, the selfies they take often focus on their physical features and fail to capture their important moments, experiences, struggles, and successes. All of this poses a particular problem for kids: how to make responsible decisions about their own digital identities.

THE MISSION: GO ON A SELFIE ADVENTURE

Posting selfies is a form of visual storytelling. Our students' photograph collections illustrate their personal narratives. Years later when they scan over those collections, they should be able to recall events, trips, feelings, and achievements. This mission encourages students to take selfies that capture not just their physical features but also their important moments, experiences, struggles, and successes. To complete this mission, students must take selfies that meet different challenges. Each challenge shows students how to capture better selfies that more effectively tell the stories of their lives. Each selfie also guides young content creators to build a strong digital identity.

Provide at least five criteria for this selfie mission. Possible challenges include taking a selfie with a pet, a favorite book, a favorite teacher, a hobby, or a favorite food. Instruct students to take selfies at different times of the day, in different environments, and engaged in different learning experiences: playing outside, exploring a new place, pointing out a geometric shape, completing a science experiment, investigating a new habitat, or representing vocabulary words. Invite them to include an "usie," a group selfie. When students complete their selfies, they will share their adventures with peers in a presentation or digital story.

We must motivate kids to reflect on what makes them unique and to experience life as individuals no matter how their peers perceive them. It's important to humanize their digital experiences and help them make responsible decisions about the ways they define themselves through digital images.

MISSION PREP

Before students go on their selfie adventures, help them reflect on the culture and history of selfies with the following activities:

- **Analyze the first selfie.** Many of us believe selfies are a new cultural trend. You and your students might be surprised to discover that chemist Robert Cornelius took the first known selfie in 1839 (see

Image 2.1). You can find this selfie in the public domain on Wikimedia Commons. Present this selfie to students along with the questions in the Mission Toolkit (see Kit 2) to provoke discussion and encourage deeper analysis of selfies.

Image 2.1: The first known selfie,
taken by Robert Cornelius.

- **Reflect on the narrative that selfies present.** Social networks display our photos as collections in chronological order. These collections capture moments of our lives and reveal our personal narratives to our online communities. Inspire students to reflect on the narratives their selfies present and to live the next chapter of their lives more meaningfully. Play the video, Around the World in 360 Degrees, which portrays the three-year travels of social media celebrity Alex Chacon. Alex is the author of the famous travel blog, ModernMotoDiaries.com, where you will find his epic video selfie adventure and his reflections about each selfie. Present this video along with the questions in the Mission Toolkit (see Kit 3) to spark discussion and reflection.

- **Explore animal selfies.** Some of the most popular selfies are with animals. Students of all ages find animal selfies fun and silly, but such selfies can also share valuable information. Instruct students to conduct an image search for the query, "animal selfies" on a safe search engine, and choose three of their favorite animal selfies to investigate. They can learn about the animal's habitat, characteristics, diet, and life.

- **Encourage students to share the apps they use to take and post selfies.** Students demonstrate for their peers the features, tools, and filters they use to make their selfies more interesting. Then they can proudly share their favorite appropriate selfies and explain what they like most about them.

MISSION LAUNCH

Step 1: Give at least five selfie challenges.

Use this task as a get-to-know-you activity or to encourage students to find real-world examples of what they are learning. For example, an English teacher who wants students to gain insight about a novel might challenge students to take selfies that reflect the fashion of the time, cultural norms, themes, politics, or the setting. If you teach math, challenge students to take selfies of numbers, fractions, geometric shapes, or angles. If you teach science, challenge students to take selfies of different states of matter, the chemical elements, or illustrations of a theory.

Present the selfie challenge to students and allow them to use props, green screens, or apps to fulfill the challenges. To protect the identity of younger learners, you may want to prompt them to create a selfie adventure for a character or puppet.

Step 2: Show them your example.

Present your own selfie adventure, which shows you completing the challenges. Your selfie challenge will help students get to know you. They love it when teachers step out of their comfort zones and lead by example. Another option is to present the selfie adventure of your pet. You are welcome to show younger learners my video of the characters Robot and Hello Kitty going on a selfie adventure. Find the video on YouTube by searching for "Adventures of Robot and Hello Kitty." The video shows the characters exploring Slovenia and Croatia.

Step 3: Teach basic photography skills.

One goal of this mission is to show students how to take different types of selfies that focus less on their physical features and more on capturing the moment. Encourage them to experiment with their cameras' capabilities – such as the timer feature and different angles and distances – and then examine the results. Ask if students are aware of the grid concept, which divides the screen into nine equal parts. Professional photographers use the grid to follow a basic composition principle known as the rule of thirds, placing the main subjects of the photo along the intersections of the gridlines to make the photo extra visually appealing.

Experimenting with the camera improves the quality of student photographs for better visual storytelling. Additionally, students learn the important concept of how different techniques change their digital identities.

Step 4: Present the selfie adventures and reflect on the journey.

Provide students with a few days or a week to complete these challenges on their own time. I would assign this mission on a Monday and give them until Friday to present their selfie adventures. Discover other strategies for extending your EdTech missions to students' homes in *Hacking Homework: 10 Strategies That Inspire Learning Outside the Classroom*. Students then present their completed selfie challenges to their peers as a slide presentation or digital story. This presentation helps students reflect on the visual stories of their selfie adventures. On the Hack Learning website, find a Selfie Adventure PowerPoint template that students can edit.

OVERCOMING MISSION OBSTACLES

Here are ideas for overcoming obstacles that might crop up in this mission.

What if students and parents don't see the value of this mission? Some may think taking selfies is silly or narcissistic, and a bunch of wasted time. Prepare an email or letter ahead of time that outlines the objectives students will achieve by launching their selfie adventures. These include helping students reflect on how they portray and define themselves online, using technology to create digital stories, and connecting class lessons to the selfie challenges. You might even include a brief explanation of the long-term ramifications of students creating negative digital identities and how this mission sheds light on the problem and helps students understand the value of positive digital identities.

How do I ease concerns of those who may feel uncomfortable sharing personal photographs? Make sure you talk to all shareholders about the objectives of this mission. Students do not need to post their selfie adventures online. Instead, they can present them to their peers as a class presentation. If you decide to have students post online, be sure parents provide written permission. Many schools have parents sign an Acceptable Use Policy that outlines the safety precautions to protect students online, the digital tools and how they are used, the student code of conduct when using technology, and the consequences when students do not follow the codes of conduct.

If a parent does not give consent, then the teacher knows before assigning the mission and can adapt this mission to make sure every student can participate. For those who are not allowed to show their faces in photographs, they can add stickers to their faces or wear a fun mask. Apps like SnapChat, Facebook, and Twitter have stickers and effects you can add to disguise faces. Showing one's face is not a requirement for this mission.

What if a student is too shy or introverted to share selfies? Again, students may choose to use masks or digital stickers for this reason. Also, some students may feel that sharing selfies with their peers leaves them vulnerable to bullying and makes them feel unsafe. To help ensure all students feel safe and secure accomplishing this mission, address bullying in advance with the entire class. The Common Sense Media Organization has many resources to address bullying and digital citizenship with your students.

What if a web tool has an age requirement? Teachers need to take precautions when having students aged thirteen years and younger share pictures of themselves online. Many web tools, apps, and social sites do not allow individuals thirteen years and younger to post images of themselves. Read the Terms and Conditions before using an app or web tool to make sure it allows students to post their selfie adventures. Remember, you can complete this mission without posting the photos online.

THE MISSION IN ACTION

During my time in Venezuela, I sent an auditorium of more than 100 language learners and their teachers on a selfie adventure. I challenged them with these seven selfie themes: an usie, a selfie showing a different perspective, a selfie with a teacher, a silly selfie, a selfie showing a special talent, a selfie in nature, and a photobomb selfie. The students worked in small groups to complete the mission.

Even though I had led this mission before with several groups of teens, university students, and their teachers throughout Venezuela, this was the first time I had a student ask me if she could be exempt from the mission. She explained that she was an introvert and did not feel comfortable taking pictures of herself. She had never taken or posted a selfie online and didn't believe that taking selfies would help her learn anything valuable. I told the student that I could understand her shyness but asked her if she could attempt the task and seek help from her peers.

At the end of the day, the student approached me. She was crying what I soon learned were tears of joy, and expressed her gratefulness for the selfie adventure. She said the activity helped her meet new friends and have a fun time with them. She learned a lot about herself and felt positive about seeing herself in photographs. Before this activity, she had never enjoyed the experience of being in photographs, but the selfie adventure gave her an encouraging experience and helped her step out of her comfort zone and engage with her peers.

So often, what our students do and share digitally impacts who they are and what they do in the physical world. After completing this mission, they will see themselves in personal adventures they captured digitally, meeting different challenges and undergoing the emotions and obstacles of each one. They will capture memories that involve their ideas, choices, and peers. They will see themselves doing things that move beyond their bedrooms or typical environments, thus building confidence and perspective. They will experience stepping out of their comfort zones and learning in different ways. Now, that's a mission worth completing!

MISSION 3

CREATE A FICTIONAL SOCIAL MEDIA PROFILE

Manage Your Digital Footprint More Purposefully

We are all leaving digital trails behind us, as we make our way around our individual lives.
– JER THORP, CO-FOUNDER OF THE OFFICE FOR CREATIVE RESEARCH / ARTIST

THE PROBLEM: STUDENTS DON'T UNDERSTAND THAT THEIR DIGITAL FOOTPRINTS SHAPE THEIR FUTURES

I ESTABLISHED MY DAUGHTER's digital footprint well before she was born, and the families of many of our young students likely have done the same. I posted my sonograms and shared highlights of my pregnancy with friends and family on social networks or through texts. I did this carefully and with trepidation. I have come to realize that even if I never posted pictures or status updates about my daughter, she still has little control over what her friends or others post about her. What they post will affect her emotionally and psychologically.

She is now starting to establish a positive footprint on her own, which we will monitor and help to guide her through. This way she makes smart choices about what she shares and her digital behavior. When she does encounter the dangers of the internet, she will have the confidence, skills, and support to overcome them.

Many schools filter and ban social media to avoid having students encounter the dark side of the internet on their watch. This means our learners are navigating the vast digital world with no guidance or support. Many already encounter the dark side of social media, such as bullying, trolling, spamming, and access to questionable content. If we don't teach them the skills to deal with these situations effectively, they may be emotionally and psychologically scarred. They may also make poor choices, which can destroy their reputations and hinder their dreams.

THE MISSION: MANAGE THE SOCIAL MEDIA PROFILE OF A HISTORICAL FIGURE

In Mission 2, our students crafted a confident digital identity with their selfie adventures – a critical early step in becoming better digital citizens and managing digital reputations. They also evaluated how social media shares and interactions impede or facilitate their future happiness, wellness, and success. This mission deepens conscientious reflection on the digital world by prompting students to create fictional social media accounts.

What if historical figures communicated with other significant figures on social media? Would their exchanges further or hinder their contributions to the world? In this mission, your learners explore the answers to these questions by taking on the roles of different historical figures who follow and interact with each other on a social network. Students create social media profiles for the historical figures, and manage the posts, shares, and exchanges for at least five days. Their choices will either enhance or sully the credibility and reputation of their historical figures. After this experiment, students determine if their shares, posts, reactions, and behavior hindered their historical figures' contributions to the world.

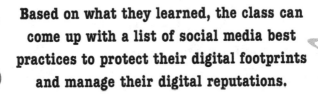

Based on what they learned, the class can come up with a list of social media best practices to protect their digital footprints and manage their digital reputations.

Your learners gain the most value by creating a fictional social media profile on a popular social network, such as Facebook, Twitter, or Instagram. These social networks model the real-world challenges digital learners face with effectively managing their own digital reputations. In the section, Overcoming Mission Obstacles, find tips for getting leadership and parents to embrace social media. In case you aren't able to use social media, students can create their profiles on Fictitious Social Media (FISM), a fake social network created just for this mission! Find the FISM Network Template in the Mission Toolkit (see Kit 4). Learn how it works in the Mission Launch section below.

MISSION PREP

At this point in our learners' development, they treasure their friendships and are seeking acceptance from their peers. Most are still defining their values and beliefs and finding themselves. Because of the influences of peer pressure and acceptance, poor digital choices may arise from time to time. The following activities help our learners to review the values they project with their digital use, while also providing an engaging opportunity to discover the values and traits of historical figures.

- **Play the Digital Trails Icebreaker.** Divide your class into pairs, and instruct students to sit facing their partners. Set a timer for two minutes. When the timer starts, the pairs converse about a question related to their digital use, and the values displayed on the overhead projector or written on the board. Find a list of suggested questions in the Mission Toolkit (see Kit 5). Go over a handful of questions beforehand so students understand the personal nature of the inquiry. Encourage them to share only what they feel comfortable sharing and to refrain from naming others or providing specific details of incidents. Remember, we want to promote personal reflection versus gossip. When the timer stops, your students switch partners and repeat the activity. Play as long as you want.

- **Analyze the impact of your digital footprint on social networks.** Distribute the Digital Footprint Investigation handout (see Kit 6). In the top row, students list two social networks they belong to. If they don't belong to social networks, they can evaluate the social media profile of a celebrity. Students answer questions regarding their top posts and shared media on each platform. The information they provide includes the number of friends or followers, the top post, the amount of likes and shares, and the personal information shared. Emphasize that this is a discussion, not a contest to see who has the highest numbers. Discuss how social media use is a personal decision and the numbers depend on each person's preferences, types of posts, online circles, and digital activity levels.

- **Google your historical figure.** One way to monitor your digital footprint is to regularly Google yourself. Many of our learners are too young to receive results, but this task becomes more necessary as they mature into professional adults. Google themselves, Google their historical figures, and compare the results.

  Next, distribute the Historical Figure Traits Map (see Kit 7). Students conduct an internet search of their historical figures, and complete the fields such as their contribution, family life, professional life, important events, and interests and quirks. At the center of the map, each student posts an image or drawing of their historical figure and lists the name and birthdate. The information in this map assists them in managing the social media accounts of their historical figures.

MISSION LAUNCH

Step 1: Fill in basic profile information for the historical figure.

Walk students through the process of registering and creating social profiles for their historical figures. If you aren't using a social network, distribute the FISM Network Template, located in the Mission Toolkit (see Kit 4). Urge students to review their Historical Figure Traits Map (see Kit 7) to help them get into character.

Next, students complete the basic profile information for their characters. Image 3.1 illustrates an example FISM profile of Albert Einstein. The first square is for a profile pic. Add the name, bio, location, and birth date in the boxes provided, and add the names of the other historical figures in the smaller boxes alongside the profile pic. The other figures along the top of the image are Einstein's fictional social media friends, and they interact with him in the comments.

If you are planning to use the FISM in your class, Google Docs is a great location for the template because it mocks the use of social media. Another option is for students to complete the template with pen and paper. Students may want to add a Creative Commons picture (see Mission 4 for details about Creative Commons), which they can find using Wikimedia Commons. If one isn't available, they can draw the image.

Image 3.1: Einstein's FISM Profile

Step 2: Post a few status updates.

Urge students to continue researching their historical figures. They will discover facts and insights that will make great status updates and count toward the required minimum of two per day. The status updates reveal the character's home life, professional life, interests, and idiosyncrasies. See Image 3.1 for an example of Einstein's status updates in a FISM profile. In one post, he announces his new hair trim, compliments of his wife. In another, he shares a video of modern-day violinist and performer Lindsey Stirling, which aligns with his love for playing the violin. Another post shares news that he submitted his doctoral thesis. All of these status updates align with actual events and knowledge about his personal and professional life. Encourage students to include photos, links, and videos in their posts.

Step 3: Collect likes and comments from classmates on the social network.

The purpose of liking and hearting in this mission is different than in actual social media. In this mission, students click like if they feel a post is believable for the character. This encourages students to post as their characters, and not as themselves. The FISM Network Template (Kit 4) provides a few spaces for peers to react to their colleagues' posts. Students like a post by adding a star (asterisk), and respond the way they believe their historical figures would respond. They might even leave comments that include quotes by their historical figures. Feel free to add more space for comments.

Step 4: Contribute to the social network for several days.

Students continue posting to social media or to the FISM network as their historical figures at least two times a day, and comment on two peers' posts each day. They continue managing the social media profile for at least five days, although more time is preferable. Remember, students post during their free time so this activity requires minimal class time.

For the first two days, try to resist providing restrictive guidelines on how to write posts and comments, including guidelines on grammar, spelling, or content. We want the social network to resemble as close to an actual social network as possible. This will create teachable moments for students to reflect on the consequences of their choices both for their historical figures and for their own, real digital footprints.

Step 5: Highlight and discuss inappropriate or problematic communication.

Check the social network daily to make sure you highlight and address any problems immediately. Point out inappropriate posts or comments to the class, but don't embarrass the student. Such examples provide an opportunity for the class to reflect on netiquette. Together, reflect on how that behavior might have had a real-world impact on the historical figure's life and contributions. Where would we be without these contributions? How might bad digital choices prevent us from making a difference? This is also a good time to provide tips for crafting better status updates and comments. Conduct an online search for "tips for good comments." Also, discuss with students how word choices, bad grammar, or misspelling impact their characters professionally.

Step 6: List best practices for social media use.

When the mission ends, host a class discussion for students to reflect on what they learned. Talk about how their use of social media impacts their ability to achieve their dreams and make a meaningful contribution in the world. Based on what they learned, the class can come up with a list of social media best practices to protect their digital footprints and manage their digital reputations. Turn these guidelines into an infographic or poster to display on the class website or in the classroom.

OVERCOMING MISSION OBSTACLES

This mission helps teachers guide students to make better choices when using social media. School leadership, administrators, and parents may try to avoid student access to social media altogether to protect kids from the dangers of cyberspace. Unfortunately, this means students might experience scary situations on social media without knowing how to effectively deal with them. The following tips will help you with the pushback.

Will this mission encourage children to join social networks? Some parents are cautious about exposing their children to social networks and may think this mission encourages it. Assure parents in advance that their children won't post any of their own information or photos, but will be sharing as historical figures. Create an information package or website for parents, highlighting the mission's essential skills and objectives, such as vital internet safety and citizenship skills to prepare children to deal with the dangers of the internet. You might include an infographic or research from the Common Sense Media Organization, illuminating the values of teaching these skills, and the consequences of not teaching them. At the end of the mission, share the profiles and the Social Media Best Practices list (from Step 6) to help parents feel better about their children creating social media profiles for historical figures.

What if my school bans social media? Many schools ban access to social networks. You may want to take on the role of working to convince school administrators or Information Technologists to lift the ban. The following suggestions will increase your chances of lifting the ban:

- Provide leadership with the details of the mission, as you did for parents.

- Inform leadership that students will not provide their personal information, but instead post as historical figures.

- Only request access to the social network you are using to complete this mission.

- Set accounts to "private" so they only allow students to access and post on each other's streams.

- Suggest lifting the ban only for the duration of the project.

- Present the skills gained during this mission, including vital internet safety and citizenship skills that students need to navigate cyberspace intelligently and safely.

I want to use social media, but isn't this too risky? Using actual social media to carry out this mission provides a more valuable learning experience; however, you can always use the Fictitious Social Media (FISM) network instead. Another idea is to use an educational social networking tool such as Google Classroom, Edmodo, or Schoology. If you do use real social media, set the social network profiles to private and instruct students to only add their classmates as friends or followers.

THE MISSION IN ACTION

Kelly Jake Duncan teaches ESL at Splendora High School in Splendora, Texas. While working in literature circles with small groups of intermediate to advanced English learners, he assigned students to take on the roles of characters from the books they were reading. One group read *Sammy and Juliana in Hollywood* by Benjamin Alire Sáenz. The book takes place in Las Cruces, New Mexico, during the late 1960s. Kelly shared numerous resources throughout the course to provide context to the events of the story and aid comprehension. These resources ranged from playing a video of "Can't Take My Eyes Off You" by Frankie Valli and The Four Seasons, to delving into the reasons for Vietnam War protests.

Students created exchanges between the characters with fake Facebook posts, Twitter posts, and text messages – as if the characters existed in the present day. The students enjoyed the book and were proud of the ways their characters interacted in the fake posts and texts. They asked if they could extend the assignment and create actual Twitter accounts for their characters to provide inspiration for other students who would read the book next year, and they did!

In addition to posting on behalf of the characters, students interacted with each other on Twitter just as the characters did in the book. They found that they were not only supporting others in Mr. Duncan's courses, they were inspiring learners and readers of the book around the world. Accounts for other characters that appeared in the book began to message them on Twitter. Also, a student created a hashtag for others to easily follow along with the characters.

The students began with no expectations aside from sharing the fake social media assignment and making their work public, but the project was so engaging that it took on a life of its own. They realized that what they do at school and on their own have a profound impact on others around the world. Their work had value and deserved to be heard. Their voices were not just worthy; they were important.

Students base most of their digital choices on enhancing their reputations in the present. Will their photos or shares get them immediate likes, positive comments, approval or acceptance? Their futures aren't a priority, but they need to realize that their decisions now will diminish or enhance their significant contributions to the world in the future. We need our learners' online behavior to align with their values and beliefs in the physical world.

Many schools ban rather than embrace social media use and instruction. As a result, our kids are facing overwhelming situations without guidance or support from adults. They want to be accepted and valued, and this motivates their digital actions. Learning is tough enough for our children who also deal with cyberbullying, sexting, and other dangers. The education system has a duty to assist kids in their development as productive members of society who live meaningful lives. Social media, our digital relationships, and our online communities play a major role in our lives. We need to welcome social media in our schools and ensure that we provide our students with strategies to stay on the light side of the internet. This mission helps to lay the groundwork for social impact and responsibility.

MISSION 4

REMIX LEARNING INTO A DIGITAL TEXTBOOK
Produce and Publish an Engaging Online Book

Lovers of print are simply confusing the plate for the food.
— DOUGLAS ADAMS, ENGLISH AUTHOR / NOVELIST

THE PROBLEM: USERS DON'T CREATE THE CURRICULUM

HISTORY, LITERATURE, SCIENCE, math, and learning in general are rich with action, conflict, imagination, and creativity. Kids love all that, so why aren't some students excited about learning? The problem isn't that students don't want to learn – they want to have input in what they learn and how they learn it. Currently, our students have little say in what we teach, how we teach, and how we assess. They don't get to decide on the content or design of their textbooks. School systems create the curriculum through policy, and teachers and school leaders primarily decide how to deliver the curriculum, as well as the content and frequency of testing.

When students adapt content and use it in their own digital creations, we call this remixing – an important part of producing new, original learning material while respecting copyrights.

We expect students to learn in the same way (which may not be the way they would choose) from the time they are toddlers all the way until they become adults. If students can't contribute to the curriculum and personalize what they learn, they are mere bystanders of their learning. They don't own the learning because we force it upon them. They aren't engaged because we don't show how the learning impacts them. It's time we let our students make choices about the instructional materials and class content.

THE MISSION: CONTRIBUTE TO A DIGITAL TEXTBOOK

Fortunately, today's technology empowers us to leave old-school practices behind. Students now have the tools to create their own digital textbooks, full of engaging content from current and past experts. Sure, our students can consume oceans of existing digital content, but creating a digital book of their own teaches them invaluable skills they can apply to an array of projects and professions. It also introduces them to the value of copyright and attribution.

For this mission, students act as contributing authors to the class digital textbook and make it available on multiple platforms and devices. Students get to design part of the textbook in the way that is most engaging to them, and demonstrate their subject knowledge in the process. For example, children might choose to include colorful, animated characters that present the material through songs or games. Older students might create books that demonstrate theories with 3D images or illustrate real-world examples of principles through interactive images, GIFs, and videos. They may want to include infographics or podcasts.

The digital textbook will include relevant content and primary resources created by others, and this is an excellent way for learners to better understand how to integrate and use other people's content efficiently and appropriately. We have unlimited access to content. Many libraries and organizations have released historical content into the public domain. When students adapt content and use it in their own digital creations, we call this remixing – an important part of producing new, original learning material while respecting copyrights.

MISSION PREP

Our students' digital textbooks should reflect their own knowledge of the content but also help others learn the topic in an engaging way. This means students need to reflect on the design of their textbooks and incorporate content from different sources. Learners must know where to find content that is licensed to use in other places. Consider these activities for helping students design a digital textbook that follows academic standards and copyright law.

- **Imagine the possibilities of digitizing a chapter.** As a class, explore a chapter in the existing printed textbook, and identify ways the textbook highlights information and assesses readers. This may include bold print, vocabulary lists, headers, images, captions, interesting facts, charts, questions, or exercises. Ask your students, "What if we turned this chapter into a digital book? How would you make the content more exciting and engaging?" Students will likely surprise you with many possibilities that go beyond integrating a quiz. Encourage them to imagine all types of additions, including learning games and augmented-reality activities.

- **Map out examples.** Together, come up with a list of subtopics or examples tied to the topic. Each student chooses one of these subtopics or examples to explore further in a mind map (written or digital). Students start by writing down their topics of exploration in the middle of a page and drawing a circle around the topic to emphasize it. Then students draw lines from the main topic to at least five to ten key facts they discover by conducting online research. Direct them to summarize each key fact in one sentence and to include the URL where they found the information.

- **Turn students into skilled searchers.** It's invaluable for students to be skilled searchers who understand how search engines work, come up with the right search terms, and know how to gather results from credible sources. Instruct students to open up their browsers to a search engine and conduct a general search about their topics. They should scan the first page of results and read the link descriptions to determine how many of the results will provide them with relevant information. Tell students they will conduct another search, but this time they should come up with better search terms for more relevant results.

  Show them search functions and features. On many search engines and databases, you can add a minus sign before a word to eliminate results with that word. Some include the ability to type "- wiki" to eliminate results from Wikipedia. Adding the plus sign will help students find content with all of the search terms. Adding quotation marks returns results with a specific phrase. Invite students to test these functions and evaluate the results.

- **Help students inspect the sources of their information.** Instruct them to click on one of the links in their search results and inspect the information source. They should determine if the information comes from a credible organization or expert in the field, if the content contains research or references, and if the videos or images are from the source or created by others.

- **Investigate Creative Commons (CC) licenses.** Our learners often enhance their own productions and creations with music, images, and content made by others. Unfortunately, much of this content is copyrighted. We can help students remix content from others responsibly by introducing them to Creative Commons content. These materials have been produced by others and licensed for free reuse, and students can find them on websites such as Wikimedia Commons, the Creative Commons database, and ccMixter. Conduct a search for CC content to use in the digital textbooks and investigate the licensing permissions using the Handout of Licensing Information (see Kit 8) located in the Mission Toolkit. Direct students to search for an image, GIF, sound file, or video clip that highlights the topic, and then list the URL, license, restrictions, and attribution.

MISSION LAUNCH

Step 1: Review formatting and layout guidelines.

Your students are ready to create their chapters to contribute to the class digital textbook. In the Mission Prep, students chose their topics and conducted preliminary research in a mind map. The next step is to familiarize themselves with the digital book creator and formatting guidelines. To add uniformity and organization to the textbook, provide students with a template to easily add their chapter details. A digital textbook template for designing a book on Google Slides is available at bit.ly/booktemplateshelly. This template includes a cover page, table of contents linked to each chapter, and a layout for student chapters. You may want to allocate two pages per student and two different layouts for their chapters (see examples in Kit 9 of the Mission Toolkit).

Google Slides is a great option to use as the digital book creator. With Slides, multiple students can work on their chapters in the document at the same time. An additional benefit is that students can include YouTube videos, GIFs, charts, graphs, and drawings to their pages. They can also design interactive images by adding transitions. When the digital textbook is complete, download it as a PDF file for offline use. Learn more about teaching with Google Slides in *Hacking Google for Education*.

Step 2: Access the template and begin the first drafts.

Students begin their chapters by listing three to five key points or questions that readers will explore. Encourage students to use their mind maps to help develop these points and the best ways to highlight them. After doing so, students will be ready to fill in the various sections of their chapters. Give them a fair amount of freedom in deciding where to include text and media. Make sure they add captions to any media, along with the link and attribution information. The last part of the chapter template includes a section for students to list references to any information they paraphrased.

Step 3: Create interactive activities.

Part of the template requires students to include two interactive exercises. Within Google Slides, students can include polls using Poll Everywhere or create interactive images by using the animations feature. They can also insert visual writing prompts into their chapters. If students create a learning game or activity on another website, they can include a clickable screenshot to lead readers directly to the activity.

Students may want to sprinkle in engaging content such as QR codes (Quick Response barcodes), containing digital information. These small, black-and-white squares are found in books, on products, coupons, restaurant menus, and magazines. When someone scans the QR code with a free QR code reader app, the app whisks the mobile device screen directly to a source that contains the answer to a question, an audio file, video, website, or a file to download. Students can create QR codes with web tools and apps, such as i-nigma, QuickMark, Visualead, Unitag, QRstuff, and the Cloud QR app. Learn more about using QR codes and other teacher tools in the book *Hacking Engagement Again*.

Step 4: Submit the chapter for peer feedback.

When students finish their chapters, it's time for the peer review process. They invite their classmates to provide feedback on the design, activities, and presentation of the content. Peers try to find answers to the key questions at the beginning of the chapters, and click on the reference links to make sure the sources are credible. Students then review and consider the feedback, and make improvements to their chapters.

Step 5: Choose the right Creative Commons license for the eBook.

As a class, use the licensing tool located on the Creative Commons website to generate a CC license image to include at the front of the book. Students decide on the options, and a license is automatically generated along with an image showing the license type.

Step 6: Publish and share the digital book.

Publish the eBook and share the final publication with family members and the school staff. You can email the link or embed the slides into a website. Also make use of the book in class. Give students a time frame to read their peers' chapters and complete the interactive activities. Not only will students learn content, but they will take pride in seeing others learn from their creation.

OVERCOMING MISSION OBSTACLES

This mission's objective is to support student ownership of learning by allowing students to make decisions about course content. This is new territory for many teachers. The following suggestions will help you face the challenges.

How do you prevent students from encountering inappropriate content while conducting searches? Parents may express concern about the possibility that this activity will expose their children to inappropriate content. Limit this risk by encouraging students to use search engines, such as Kiddle, Safe Search Kids, Kid's Search, KidzSearch, and Kid Rex. Another idea is to provide your students with a list of recommended websites and databases. In the Mission Prep section, you will find examples of safe websites where students can find Creative Commons content appropriate for educational settings.

Are there problems with other book creation tools? You have plenty of choices when it comes to digital publishing. Children can create colorful books with fun characters using Little Bird Tales, ToonDoo, or My Storybook. Older students can design sophisticated digital books using WikiJunior, Wikibooks, Book Creator, or iBook Author. I suggest Google Slides, but feel free to use any digital book creator to complete this mission, just be sure the platform allows you to download a copy of the digital book. If it doesn't, then all of your students' work on the digital textbook will disappear! Note also that platforms may require students to create accounts, and may not offer the collaborative features of Google Slides.

How do you ensure that students read the other chapters? One option is to grade a student-designed interactive activity. Students can design assessments using Google Forms, and automatically share the grades spreadsheet with you. Another option is to have students take a screenshot showing they completed the interactive activity, and turn it in to earn credit.

THE MISSION IN ACTION

André Spang is one of Germany's most celebrated teachers, recognized for getting teenagers to use technology with a focus on

21st century skills – creativity, communication, collaboration, and critical thinking. One of André's most impressive student projects involved a religion class publishing a multimedia digital textbook, entitled, "Eucharistie – wenn nicht jetzt, wann dann" ("The Eucharist – If Not Now, Then When"). See Image 4.1 for an example page of the student-created textbook.

Image 4.1: Sample page from the student textbook, "Eucharistie – wenn nicht jetzt, wann dann?"

Religion is a subject that requires more personal exploration than just learning from a textbook. Creating digital texts gave André's students the opportunity to examine the subject in a personal way. To prepare the content, nearly sixty students used Wikibooks, which, as the name suggests, functions similarly to Wikipedia. Wikibooks allows an unlimited number of authors to edit a Wiki page collaboratively online, and users can easily create text with images, videos, apps, and audio files.

Students first studied about the Eucharist in the classroom. Then they worked on putting that information in their own words in the Wikibook. Wiki collaboration features helped students map out the book collaboratively since they allow anyone in the group to edit the pages at any time. Wiki saves updates and makes them visible to others who access the pages from any computer. As André's students worked, they viewed edits and restored previous versions if they made mistakes.

Once content work had wrapped up on Wikibooks, André decided to use the iBooks Author software to publish the finished digital book. iBooks Author supports audio, video, surveys, and graphics, all features André's students had used or at least explored. Students worked together throughout the publishing phase, and they submitted their finished work to a nationwide religious digital-learning competition in Germany.

This project supported the safe and competent use of digital media and technology, which André argues is a prerequisite for participating in and shaping a digital society. His students reported being motivated to learn religion by creating their own digital books versus learning in a traditional way. Students enjoyed integrating different types of media into an open source book to share worldwide. Additionally, the students were excited about collaborating with a large group of peers through Wiki, Facebook groups, and other digital tools. To teach others about religion, they enhanced their video, audio, text, images, and game skills, and they gained expertise in image licensing, software apps, and widgets.

One reason our students cherish technology and the internet in the classroom is because they are in charge of their learning. They choose engaging media to explore, such as apps, videos, GIFs, games, and podcasts. This mission invites students to take charge of their learning by remixing the work of others and combining that with some of their own ideas into a digital textbook. As they complete the steps, they learn to respect copyright and appropriately attribute the work of others.

MISSION 5

DEBATE ISSUES, DON'T DISS PEOPLE

Argue Differences of Opinion Respectfully

*Debate and divergence of views can only
enrich our history and culture.*
— IBRAHIM BABANGIDA, FORMER PRESIDENT OF NIGERIA

THE PROBLEM: ONLINE ARGUMENTS RESULT IN PERSONAL ATTACKS

LATELY, THE NEWS has featured the long-standing Twitter feud between President Donald Trump and the media. The public has criticized both sides for their behavior. At one point, the argument escalated and the President tweeted a GIF of himself symbolically body-slamming CNN. The news media took offense, claiming the GIF encouraged violence toward reporters; the Office of the President and Twitter disagreed. Tensions continue to rise.

This incident exemplifies the nature of many online arguments.

Children to adults share their opinions openly on social networks, but are offended when others disagree with them. They react with aggression or resort to personal attacks. All involved seem to overlook the true issues, and all parties leave the conversation upset, learning nothing new about the topic and missing a powerful opportunity for debate to open our minds and elevate our thinking.

We need to transform the digital debating mindset and help students see debate as a vehicle to strengthen their intellect and character.

The way schools teach debate doesn't align with how our learners conduct arguments in real life. Traditionally, we teach students to debate by writing argumentative or persuasive essays. While this is important, our digital learners need to engage in online debates. They need the opportunity to draft shorter arguments to share with the public, as well as practice in responding intelligently to those with opposing views. Our students may regularly debate or argue on social media, yet schools rarely afford them the opportunity to acquire respectful debate skills as part of the curriculum.

THE MISSION: ENGAGE IN A THOUGHT-PROVOKING ONLINE DEBATE

In Missions 2 and 3, your students gained confidence in defining their digital identities and became aware of how their posts and shares impacted their digital reputations. Those first steps laid the groundwork for this mission to participate in a respectful and thought-provoking virtual debate. Rich debate keeps the conversation going, celebrates differences of opinions and perspectives, and values well-constructed arguments. All involved realize how a strong opponent opens their minds, challenges their beliefs, and improves their critical thinking skills. Additionally, healthy debate fosters peace, promotes democracy, and builds community relationships.

First, our digital citizens will learn how to craft clear, persuasive, and compelling arguments for an online forum. Their arguments will state their positions, help their peers understand the reasons and logic behind their positions, and back up their views with support and evidence. Then, classmates post respectful and logical counter-arguments, which further the dialogue. Students read these counter-arguments with an open mind and revise their initial arguments with new insights. They develop strategies for dealing with abusive and hurtful comments, and learn how to passionately argue while keeping their emotions in check so they don't personally attack peers, but instead argue points of contention.

MISSION PREP

As we know, online debates escalate quickly and bring out the worst in people. Young people may question the value of spending their time listening to beliefs and opinions different from their own, and they may attack the individual instead of logically rebutting specific points. The activities below prepare learners to approach varying opinions with an open mind and focus their arguments on the issues.

- **Confront fears, myths, and intolerance.**
  Anonymously poll students on their attitudes

toward participating in respectful debates. Find a list of possible questions for the poll in the Mission Toolkit (see Kit 10). Present the poll results and host a discussion about tolerance, open-mindedness, and how differences help us grow and progress.

- **Play the agree/disagree warm-up.** Students must take a stand on issues to be skilled debaters. Use masking tape to create a line on your classroom floor. Line students up on the left side of the tape, facing you. State a claim, such as, "Dogs are better pets than cats." Instruct students to remain standing on the left side of the line if they agree and to move to the right side if they disagree. Students then face their peers. Starting on the left, each student gives one reason to support the claim. Then students on the right give reasons that dispel the claim. Continue this activity with safe topics and coach students to handle increasingly intense topics.

- **At various intervals, share rules and guidelines for building a safe environment to share opinions.** Record these guidelines and tips to review later. For example, before students share their reasons why dogs are better pets than cats, state the rule that all must respect the listener. Elicit examples of how we show respect to foster understanding of the rule. After the first sharing of reasons, guide a group discussion to identify the components of strong reasoning.

- **Identify the guidelines for fostering a good online debate.** As a class, evaluate how online debates differ from face-to-face debates. Present the class with the guidelines they came up with for respecting each other during the warm-up. Determine which guidelines work for fostering a good online debate, and add additional guidelines to complete the list.

- **Improve online arguments.** Show the class an example of an online argument that went awry. The initial opinion should be strong and exemplify good writing techniques, before the conversation descends into an argument within the string of comments. Reddit's Change My View forum has great examples of strong arguments followed by good and bad counter-arguments. The arguments and comments must meet strict criteria, and the moderator pulls any comments that violate the rules. Have the class analyze the strengths and weaknesses of the arguments and come up with guidelines for their own arguments. Then have the class analyze the counter-arguments and identify the most compelling ones. They should identify what makes the counter-arguments strong and come up with guidelines for their own.

MISSION LAUNCH

Step 1: Focus arguments with a specific claim.

Instruct students to jot down ten strong, evidence-supported belief statements or viewpoints. The warm-up may inspire ideas. Have them cross out any ideas that they are tied to emotionally, that they don't care enough about, or that promote violence, hate, or discrimination. Students choose one of the remaining statements as their topic for the online debate. Help them transform their statements into specific claims that focus their arguments.

Step 2: Outline six valid reasons.

Review the qualities of strong support delineated by the class in the warm-up. Students outline a minimum of six reasons to support their claims based on these qualities and conduct a quick search of each reason to ensure its validity. They show a few peers their reasons and ask them to choose the three most persuasive and interesting before deciding on the three reasons they will include in their arguments.

Step 3: Survey people to gather insight and evidence.

Students create a survey with at least five questions to gather insight and evidence to support their claims and reasons. Help students draft clear, short, specific, and simple questions that will elicit meaningful feedback. Ask them to opt for multiple choice, open-ended, or ranking questions – and to avoid only yes/no questions. I recommend Google Forms as a tool for students to create surveys. You can learn more about teaching with Google Forms in *Hacking Google for Education*.

Step 4: Post arguments and create counter-arguments.

Students post their arguments in a designated online platform. Note that the idea isn't to post a five-page argumentative essay with scholarly resources. Think of this as a precursor to these types of essays. These online arguments should consist of three paragraphs or less in simple language, with logic, reasoning, and evidence. The idea is to spark debate, which means the arguments must appeal to their peers and be easy to digest. Your young debaters should begin to prepare their counter-arguments.

Step 5: Counter-argue and refute the counter-arguments.

Once students post their arguments, other students post counter-arguments. The counter-arguments should challenge one or two ideas made by the author and provide reasoning and support for their contentions. Writers should check the forum and refute all counter-arguments. These counter-arguments must be respectful and address the contentions with well-thought-out reasoning. Encourage students to concede on certain areas of agreement. The idea isn't to win the argument, but to refine belief systems and values. Additionally, conceding on specific areas moves the conversation forward to debate other areas of the issue, which leads to a broader understanding of the topic.

Step 6: Introduce a troll.

After a few days of healthy debate, announce to the class that a troll has snuck into their forum in an effort to thwart their missions. Trolls are individuals who target an online group and post inflammatory or off-topic messages to provoke a reaction or start quarrels. The troll doesn't want your students to gain the skills to promote healthy debate, because he wants them to join him in spreading chaos on the internet.

The troll joins the group for a day or two, and only after your students have engaged in healthy debate. Set up an account with the username Troll, and wreak havoc in all threads so no one feels singled out. Your class troll will not name call, use inappropriate language, bully, or do anything that would hurt your relationship with your students. Instead, the troll might make outrageous claims about the argument, post the same message multiple times, ask silly questions, or spam the thread with nonsense.

Step 7: Come up with strategies to end the troll's havoc.

Students must come up with strategies to effectively handle the troll and limit his destruction. Allow students to search the web for tips using the query, "deal with trolls" and test these strategies. Often, trolls suffer from mental illness and the best way to deal with them is to limit engagement. Other tips include reporting them, blocking, and muting. Eventually, the troll gets bored and moves on to the next victim.

Step 8: Reconstruct arguments with new perspectives.

Students use the Final Post Template (available in Kit 11 of the Mission Toolkit) to complete their final posts, and highlight three or more peer statements that made them think deeply about their topics. They should identify statements that incited them, challenged their thinking, pointed out ideas they didn't address, directed them to interesting research, or introduced them to a new experience. The students quote each peer's statement and describe what they learned from it. Finally, they conclude their post by revisiting their initial stance and describing what has changed.

OVERCOMING MISSION OBSTACLES

A compelling counter-argument opens our minds and helps us refine our values and beliefs. In order to facilitate rich debate, students must focus on the issues, and see the tremendous value of a worthy opponent. Meet these challenges head on with these strategies.

What if the debate negatively impacts peer relationships? Young people are uncomfortable with criticism, disagreement, and those who challenge their beliefs. They may feel attacked by others, especially by faceless others behind a keyboard. We need to transform the digital debating mindset and help students see debate as a vehicle to strengthen their intellect and character.

Before the debate begins, ask students to consider sports, games, or competitions. Who makes them better players – those who challenge them, or those who give them no competition and let them win? In the same way, differences of opinion and disagreement inspire deep thinking. Therefore, they should appreciate their peers who were the most challenging during the debate because their counter-arguments inspired deeper thinking. Their final posts help learners identify the peers and arguments that contributed the most to their learning. This is one way to get them to see the learning value of debates. Students may want to issue digital badges to recognize strong counter-arguments. Learn more about designing and issuing digital badges in Mission 9.

What if it becomes a heated debate? Host the debate in a private class forum that you manage, where only class members can view it – such as Canvas, Moodle, Schoology, or Edmodo. If a thread gets hot, hot, hot, limit the exposure and delete questionable content. Make sure students regularly see the guidelines the class came up with in the Mission Prep, and that you strictly enforce them. When students violate the rules, talk to the parties involved individually at first, then together. Ask them to reflect on the reasons they reacted badly and determine better choices the next time a conversation confronts them with a similar situation and feelings. Then get both parties to apologize and work things out in person.

How do we avoid misunderstandings? To sidestep misunderstandings and offending peers, advise students to avoid writing in caps, using sarcasm, launching personal attacks, sounding condescending, and over-using exclamation marks. They will want to provide specific reasons, facts, and examples to support their arguments, rather than just stating that an opposing opinion is wrong. Advise students to point out just one or two issues of contention in each counter-argument to keep the discussion as understandable and clear as possible.

THE MISSION IN ACTION

Kimberly Sanchez is the ESL and Students with Interrupted Formal Education (SIFE) teacher at an international high school exclusively for recently arrived English language learners. Kimberly and the twelfth-grade team of teachers collaboratively prepared the seniors to participate in a grand project entitled "The Great Debate."

She divided students into small groups. Each group designated one member as the group's political candidate and spokesperson. The groups conducted research on different issues backed by their candidates. Then, all the candidates presented their issues in person and debated the other candidates. They used evidence from their research to back up their points of view, counter-argue, and offer rebuttals.

To prepare for The Great Debate, Kimberly taught her students argumentation techniques by facilitating several virtual debates using SMART lab activities. Students first learned the parts of an argument and then studied "Accountable Talk." These are helpful phrases to use during a debate, such as "I agree/disagree with this because," and "I would like to add," and "I think this because," and "Can you give an example of ... "

When students were ready to practice their debating skills, Kimberly directed them to visit Classlab.com with their mobile devices or laptops, and enter the class ID number. From there, students could view a claim presented at the top of the SMART lab screen. Under the claim, the screen was divided into two columns: yes and no. Students started by choosing a side and typing a specific reason for their choice. Then those on opposing sides wrote counter-arguments or asked clarifying questions under their peers' reasons. Kimberly facilitated by providing tips to strengthen their reasoning and support, and she also helped students to reflect on their tone and language toward peers when counter-arguing.

Students participated in several of these virtual debates. Topics included: Is technology helpful or harmful? Should students be able to graduate from high school even if they don't pass their Regents exams? Should parents allow kids to date at any age they want to? Should kids be considered adults at the age of sixteen, eighteen, or twenty-one? When students didn't understand a topic, they researched it on the internet, which allowed them to learn more details about the issues.

Students enjoyed the virtual debates and The Great Debate. They felt the virtual debates helped them clarify their ideas and form strong arguments, and they valued debating with their peers who helped them better understand the issues. Students also reported that the debates introduced them to issues they'd face in the U.S., which they hadn't considered.

The ability to powerfully communicate beliefs and spark rich debate is such a rewarding skill for our digital learners. It will serve them as they take on leadership roles, and help them to realize how much they learn by surrounding themselves with diverse opinions and perspectives. They learn to value differences and appreciate their peers who push their thinking in new directions and make them more passionate about their beliefs. Seeing their peers in this new light motivates them to focus on debating issues versus destroying the people behind opposing ideas. To understand democracy and promote peace, our learners need to listen to their peers, be open-minded to their ideas, and celebrate their contributions.

MISSION 6

SEEK AND PRESERVE
THE TRUTH

Share Digital News Responsibly and Accurately

*Put it before them briefly so they will read it, clearly so they
will appreciate it, picturesquely so they will remember it and,
above all, accurately so they will be guided by its light.*
— JOSEPH PULITZER, HUNGARIAN-AMERICAN PUBLISHER / CREATOR OF THE PULITZER PRIZE

THE PROBLEM: STUDENTS DON'T CARE ABOUT
PROTECTING AND PRESERVING THE TRUTH

TWO GREAT SUPERHEROES, Superman and Spider-Man, were
journalists. They chased after truth in the name of justice
and sought to protect people by making sure the truth prevailed.
Superman and Spider-Man are still revered cultural icons, but
times have changed since they first appeared in the pages of
comic books. When their characters originated, verified media
outlets reported the news by hiring professional journalists who

upheld ethical codes and standards. News spreads much differently these days.

The internet and social media have transformed the way our students consume and value news. Our students no longer look to official news sources to learn what is happening in the world. They are more likely to piece together facts about events from several people and sources versus one official news source. Unfortunately, this means students are consuming an unhealthy amount of biased and fabricated news. Anyone with internet access can report information as news and make it engaging through blogs, captivating images, videos, and podcasts. However, most of the people sharing the news are ordinary citizens with no qualifications or training in journalism. Or worse – they may deliberately create and share untrue information to support a specific cause or view. It can be hard for students (and adults, for that matter) to tell the difference.

Our students already act as citizen journalists and reporters on social media, and they share the way they perceive events through images, videos, podcasts, and blogs. In order for our students to care about seeking and destroying fake news, we need to teach them to be responsible creators, consumers, and sharers of the news. We need to teach them how to quickly fact-check news and investigate their news sources.

THE MISSION: REPORT THE NEWS
ACCURATELY AND RESPONSIBLY

The time has come to motivate your students to guard and preserve the truth! Students collaborate with peers on a news team to seek the truth behind a story and accurately report it without bias. The news teams shoot video footage of the events and record live interviews with eyewitnesses and/or experts. They analyze the footage, cut it, and piece it together to produce a news broadcast with the key facts.

Accurately reporting the news is quite a process, and students will experience a learning curve while they improve their digital competence and usage of video recording tools.

Throughout this mission, students engage in cooperative and collaborative learning activities with technology – vital experiences missing in most curricula. As united teams, students make decisions about the way they want to present their news stories. These decisions help the teams divide the workload according to individuals' strengths and preferences. Different team members will need to fill roles responsible for conducting interviews, summarizing the story into newsbytes, capturing footage, or using video editing tools to piece the final product together. All the while, members will communicate and operate as a collective unit.

At each stage, students gain the necessary digital skills required for producing and creating with technology. For example, they will test specific tool settings or work with special effects to improve their broadcasts; enhance their technical skills working with a video camera, microphone, and teleprompters; and learn how to use video and audio editing tools to improve sound and production quality. More important, the news teams must make ethical decisions with the technology. They take all the information and footage they gathered and decide how they will present the story and add emotion. In this way, students experience firsthand the power of technology to inform and persuade an audience.

MISSION PREP

Our digital learners need insight into the important processes that professional news agencies, crews, reporters, and journalists undergo to ensure they report the news accurately. The following activities introduce learners to interviewing skills, fact checking, and the general layout of a broadcast.

- **Fact check news stories.** Open browsers to one of the following fact-checking websites: Snopes, FactCheck, or Politifact. Demonstrate how students can quickly verify facts using the search engines on these websites. Next, present a news article with faulty reporting to your students. Instruct them to identify key facts, statistics, and claims in the article; then verify them using the fact-checking website. Students share their findings and determine the negative impact of this faulty reporting. Continue this activity with at least two more news stories.

- **Analyze the real dangers of spreading fake news.** Often, students click like or repost news without a vetting process. They don't realize this contributes to the spread of fake news, because what they "like" appears in the feeds of their friends and followers. Investigate the dangers of the massive spread of mistruths by analyzing how fake news impacted the 2016 presidential elections, led to violence at a Washington pizza place (Pizzagate), and led to nuclear threats on Israel by Pakistan's then-defense minister, Khawaja Muhammad Asif. Present one of these events to your students to research the fake news source, the contributors to the false reporting, and the harmful results. Find information and teaching materials about these events on the following websites: PBS News Hour and The New York Times Learning Network.

- **Trace the source of content you share.** Ask students to identify an interesting image, video, or article that they shared or liked on one of their social network feeds. Using the Trace the Source handout (see Kit 12) located in the Mission Toolkit, students reflect on how this content spread to their newsfeeds, and their roles in spreading it further.

- **Evaluate news broadcasts.** Distribute the Evaluation Form for a News Broadcast (see Kit 13). Each student will use this form to analyze news broadcasts with fellow student reporters. Find great examples of student newscasts on the Scholastic Kid Reporters' Notebook website, the Voice K website, and the Signal to Noise Festival website (the Mission in Action section describes this festival in more detail).

MISSION LAUNCH

Step 1: Organize news teams.

Divide students into news teams of three or four members. The teams use the Newscast Team Planning handout (see Kit 14) to designate roles and responsibilities, including an interviewer/ reporter, anchor, camera person, and director. The interviewer is in charge of scheduling and recording interviews and coming up with good questions. The anchor begins and ends the newscast, shares a summary of the most important facts of the story, and introduces the interviews. (Both the interviewer and anchor are responsible for fact-checking.) The camera person captures footage of the event, works with the interviewer to capture the interviews, and records the entire broadcast. The director oversees the production, recording, and editing of the entire broadcast.

Step 2: Begin the initial investigation of the news story and plan the coverage.

Assign the news teams the topics for their news stories. They can use the internet, materials you provide, or textbooks to answer the "Who? What? Where? When? Why?" questions of their stories. This is part of the Newscast Team Planning handout (see Kit 14). The teams should fact check all answers and confirm the credibility of their sources. Based on the answers on the Planning handout, the news teams will brainstorm a list of potential people to interview and questions to ask, and outline the video footage they would like to capture. The news teams will schedule their next meeting and set a deadline to complete all the recordings and review them as a team. At this meeting, the anchor will present a news brief summarizing the key points of the story.

Step 3: Capture footage and conduct interviews.

The interviewer contacts the sources via email or phone. During this initial contact, students set up a time to conduct the live interviews, let sources know what the interview is about, provide a time frame for the interview, obtain consent to record and share the interview, and let the interviewee know who will have access to the interview. An Interview Request Email Template is available in the Mission Toolkit (see Kit 15). Once the team schedules the interviews, they can send the interviewee the questions and details about the recording process and platform.

The interviewer and the camera person will coordinate to record the interview. If the news team is covering a live event, the camera person will capture live coverage and record the live interviews. Help your students secure permission in advance to record the event, and obtain consent to use the recorded footage of people appearing in the video.

Step 4: Review the footage and plan the broadcast.

The news team meets again to review the video footage and interviews. They decide what to cut and what to keep to convey the key points of their story. The news teams should be mindful of the story they are presenting to the audience and make sure the footage and recordings accurately present the main points of the news story. After that review is complete, it's time for the news team to write the script and plan the broadcast details, such as the costumes or clothing, backdrops, and effects. They will want to post details of each scene and provide a script for the anchor. The Mission Toolkit has an Example Newscast and Script handout (see Kit 16) that you can use just for your own reference or as a sample to distribute to your class. Guide students to be as detailed as possible; however, this is just a plan and their final newscast may differ a little from this plan.

Step 5: Produce the broadcast.

Production begins! The anchor and interviewer (now the reporter) are in place and ready to go. If the news team wants to use a teleprompter to help the anchor and reporter follow the script, make sure it is also in place and ready to go. Set one up using an iPad, tablet, or have one of the team members hold up cue cards. The following sites offer free online teleprompters: FreeTeleprompter.org, Cueprompter.com, and EasyPrompter.com.

The camera person should now have the video camera set to record. The director provides instructions and oversees the overall production. Once they record the broadcast, the news team is ready to edit and add any special effects before submitting it.

Step 6: Perform the final edits.

The director pieces together the final broadcast for the news team to view. The director can edit the broadcast and add special effects with the help of a video-editing program, such as TouchCast, OpenShot, Moovly, iMovie, or Windows Movie Maker. When the news team is happy with the production, the director submits it to the teacher.

Step 7: Host a viewing of the broadcasts.

Publish the newscasts in one location for easy viewing. You can add them to a YouTube, Vimeo, or SchoolTube channel and make them viewable only by those who have the link. Send an email with a link to parents and the school staff, inviting them to view the broadcasts. In class, host a viewing party. Allow one member of each news team to briefly introduce and show the broadcast. Ideally, these video newscasts should be five minutes or less.

OVERCOMING MISSION OBSTACLES

Accurately reporting the news is quite a process, and students will experience a learning curve while they improve their digital competence and usage of video recording tools. During each stage, students and teachers will face obstacles and pushback. Here arc suggestions for meeting these challenges.

What if parents or leaders worry the broadcasts expose children's identities? Help parents realize their children are already creating and sharing digital content online, possibly without much guidance. Assure them that you will oversee the entire process. Let them know your class broadcasts will only be shared with those who have the link, and not shared publicly. You may want to consider using students' first names and last initials within the broadcasts. To further protect student identities, students can use apps such as Talking Tom and Ben News, or Tellagami, to create newscasts with virtual reporters.

How do students produce quality broadcasts? Producing a quality video recording takes effort. If recording on location, make sure the background noise doesn't drown out the reporter, the scene includes proper lighting, and the weather and scenery don't detract from the broadcast. Reporters and anchors should practice reading the news in front of the camera a few times to make sure they are speaking at a good volume and pace and that viewers can easily understand the broadcast. If they decide to use a teleprompter, definitely practice first. Remind students to dress appropriately.

Can I teach a condensed version of this mission? If you have limited time, try this condensed version. Provide the news teams with a news article to fact check. The news teams jot down the important facts and information they need to cover in a short newscast, and create scripts based on the list of facts. Instead of filming, the teams can use the apps mentioned earlier, Talking Tom and Ben News, or Tellagami, to produce quick newscasts.

THE MISSION IN ACTION

Jon Samuelson is the Innovation Strategist for the Beaverton K12 School District in Oregon. Jon works with teachers and students at the elementary, middle, and high schools to produce various creative digital projects, including video news broadcasts. At one of the elementary schools, he collaborated with a teacher and her fourth graders to produce their five-minute video newscasts called the SM News. They produced a newscast every three or four weeks with an iPad, mostly covering local school events, functions, fundraisers, and news. Sometimes the news related to a course topic. For example, when they studied mythology, students created a newscast presented by Greek Gods and Goddesses. Different students worked with Jon as news crew members during their free time, including after school and during lunch, to help produce the newscasts. They took turns fulfilling the roles of director, camera person, and interviewer.

Each newscast helped the fourth-graders gain different soft skills (interpersonal and communications) and hard skills (technical knowledge). They learned how to collaborate with peers to produce the newscast, and they learned task management, time management, and team management. With the initial broadcasts, the fourth-graders learned how to conduct interviews, create news stories, and write scripts. After they achieved these skills, they worked with Jon on improving the overall quality of their newscasts.

After each newscast, the students came together with Jon and the teacher to critique the overall production. The critiques started with students sharing positive comments, and discussing what they could do better. Such feedback led Jon to teach the student crews how to work with technology to improve the overall production. He taught them new techniques, camera angles, and editing skills. Students learned how to improve the sound quality, do shot frames, work with a green screen, and use apps to add cool effects. Jon also helped them obtain equipment and learn to use it. Students began to experiment with using books to steady the camera. Eventually, they learned how to get the best camera angles with their iPads using a tripod and hook stands, and they learned how to use lapel mics and high-quality microphones.

The students became especially enthusiastic and creative when using the green screen and the TouchCast app. Fourth-grade imaginations went wild as they added cool effects, captions, and transitions. One of the newscasts, titled "Mythology News," began with two students dressed as Athena and Hera reporting in front of the Parthenon. Then a student dressed as Persephone appeared in the next scene interviewing a student dressed as Hermes about stolen cattle. The students used TouchCast's green screen feature to superimpose the different images to the background.

The teacher emailed the videos to parents, who enjoyed watching the creativity and enthusiasm. The class submitted their newscasts to the Signal to Noise Festival, a district-wide competition celebrating creative digital productions at the elementary, middle, and high school levels. Local professionals judge the student submissions and the Signal to Noise Festival website posted the finalists' videos that were announced at an awards ceremony. Elementary school finalists included newscasts about amazing immigrants, helping homeless pets, reporting live from the school's Maker Faire, and investigating gangs with a local officer.

Every day billions of people share their observations, research, ideas, and opinions with others online through status updates, blogs, videos, and podcasts. The content students consume impacts their beliefs, actions, and maybe even voting choices. The internet inundates our students with information, and most consume it without any vetting process. This mission helps them to become responsible creators, consumers, and sharers of the news, and to take on the weight of this responsibility in a fun way. They will seek the truth as professional reporters, and be wise to the sources behind the news they consume.

MISSION 7

ASSEMBLE A GLOBAL CLASS MEETUP

Join the World Community and Discuss a Pressing Issue

If we have no peace, it is because we have forgotten that we belong to each other.
— MOTHER TERESA, NUN AND MISSIONARY

THE PROBLEM: STUDENTS LACK INTEREST IN AND UNDERSTANDING OF GLOBAL ISSUES

For FOUR YEARS, I taught and studied in Germany. Living in a different country made me realize how ethnocentric I was and how little I knew about world issues and foreign policy and relations. I became aware of my duty as an educator to help my students understand, respect, and accept a multitude of cultures.

All my classes of German students, from age four to adult, video conferenced with students from other countries and collaborated on projects. The classes had the opportunity to ask each other questions, and I admit that some of the questions asked by the American students astonished me, such as whether German students have electricity, drive cars, or know of Justin Bieber. I was nervous the questions would offend my students, but they enjoyed teaching others about their way of life and getting the opportunity to practice their English with Americans. The German students also asked surprising questions, like if everyone in Texas wears cowboy hats and boots.

These dialogues help students challenge stereotypes, overcome their discomfort, and celebrate differences.

These intercultural exchanges made such an impression on the students. However, I initiated and planned each one, not the U.S. teachers. In fact, I didn't know any teachers Skyping in the classroom or participating in global collaboration projects in any of the schools where I had worked in the U.S. and abroad. A decade later, I still rarely see global citizenship and exchanges emphasized in curricula. Our students are growing up in a connected world, and they must learn to communicate and collaborate effectively with individuals around the globe to solve world issues.

THE MISSION: COORDINATE A VIDEO MEETUP
WITH A CLASS IN A DIFFERENT COUNTRY

Kids use their digital devices to connect with individuals in other countries, but this doesn't mean they understand how to do so with an open mind, a respectful perspective, or the intent to learn something about other cultures. Most of their exchanges are on social networks where communication happens primarily through typing. Individuals don't reflect on the impact of their text-based dialogues because they don't see the human being at the other end of the conversation. Communicating with a person from a different country requires considerable reflection and advanced communication skills. It presents students with different viewpoints, languages, and beliefs, which can make them uncomfortable, scared, or even angry.

Video conferencing is more intimate and enables students from different countries to have an open dialogue. Our students see the impact of their words through the other person's facial expressions and body language. They use these nonverbal and verbal cues to guide the direction of the conversation, rephrase, clarify, and frame follow-up questions. These dialogues help students challenge stereotypes, overcome their discomfort, and celebrate differences. To complete this mission, your class will organize two video conferences with a class in a different country. The first video conference is a meet and greet where the classes will introduce themselves, their schools, and participate in a cultural exchange activity. During the second meetup, the classes join in a deeper discussion on their experiences and perspectives on a pressing global issue.

MISSION PREP

As a class, recall the insights gained in Mission 5: Debate the Issues, Don't Diss People for fostering thought-provoking dialogue. Expect students to approach the meetups with open minds, respect, and an appreciation for differences. The following activities extend these virtues to global collaboration.

- **Create an About Me poster.** Cultural acceptance begins with each other in the classroom. Students need opportunities to express their uniqueness and feel accepted and valued by their classmates. Encourage them to share their goals, likes, interests, culture, and family history in an About Me poster. Their posters may be a collage of images, quotes, stickers, and symbols that represent themselves. You may want create digital About Me posters with Canva or EduBuncee. Students present their posters to their peers and explain the meaning of the images, symbols, and words.

- **Listen to music from the country.** Play classic and current music from the partner school's country for students to enjoy. Solicit recommended artists and songs from your partner teacher. Ask students to write down the emotions they associate with the music and imagine what type of movie might feature the songs in the soundtrack. Share interesting facts about the artists and music.

- **Highlight important contributions by the country's citizens.** Show students photos representing significant contributions from the country's past and current citizens, and ask them to guess the contribution from the photo. Follow up by playing an interview or showing a photograph featuring the person. Students discuss how the contribution improved lives.

- **Take a virtual tour of the area.** Locate the school on Google Maps or Google Earth and virtually explore the area. Ask students to compare the school grounds, restaurants, the town layout, and the landscape to theirs. In pairs, they discuss the differences and imagine what life might be like for students in the partner country.

MISSION LAUNCH

Step 1: Coordinate with the partner teacher.

You and your partner teacher are ready to organize the first meetup. Decide on the video conferencing tool and use the tool to meet each other and plan the initial meet and greet. Teachers tend to use Skype and Google Hangouts. Save time and limit the email exchanges by creating a collaborative document, such as Google Docs or OneNote, to plan the details of the first meetup. In the document, include the date and time for your meetup.

Visit TimeandDate.com to help you schedule a time that works for multiple time zones. Establish a timeline to make sure you don't go past the allotted time. In the Mission Toolkit, you will find a Class Meetup Scheduling Template (see Kit 17) to help you set up the schedule for this initial meeting.

During the session, plan for student introductions, a cultural exchange activity, and a questioning period. If the classes are large, consider having students share their first names along with a picture and three fun facts about themselves on a safe and private online space, such as a password-protected Padlet. Peers will be able to see the names written down, which may be new to them. When the classes connect, students can say their names aloud so students on both sides will know how to pronounce the names.

Step 2: Plan the culture-sharing activity.

The Mission Prep activities introduced students to the culture and famous people from the partner school's country. Your class will discover more through the cultural exchange activity. This is a brief activity of ten minutes or less. Students can teach each other songs, games, dances, fingerplays, or a custom. In one of my Skype sessions, my four- to six-year-old German students learned how to create an origami box. Another idea is to show five objects to the other class, which represent foods, events, or facts about your school or area. Ask students what they would like to teach the other class to do, and practice the activity.

Step 3: Prepare a short list of interview questions.

The initial video conference also includes a questioning period. The class should prepare at least five questions to learn about the other students. Exchange the questions with the other teacher ahead of time to clarify misunderstandings and to allow students time to prepare answers. This will help to keep the meetup on schedule and within the time limit. Students might ask the other class about their favorite singers, athletes, or shows; the most popular sports; or their school routines. Keep questions short, clear, and simple to understand, because English might not be the first language.

Step 4: Arrange the classroom and the equipment.

Arrange your classroom to provide the best viewing and sound quality. Familiarize your class with the schedule of events. For the introductions, students line up and say a quick greeting in the microphone, preferably in the language of their peers, and introduce themselves. When students finish introducing themselves, direct them where to go to get ready for the cultural exchange activity. Find out the details from the partner teacher in advance, so you can prepare the best arrangement. For instance, you may need to locate one or two students near the webcam to provide instructions, while the rest of the class stands in the back to demonstrate the activity. Have a plan for quickly rearranging students (if necessary) when it comes time to learn the activity presented by the other class.

For the question session, I place one or two chairs and a microphone in front of the webcam for students to use while asking their questions. Another student can repeat the answer to the rest of the class if needed. When the partner class asks questions, the students who will answer sit in the chairs and share the prepared responses. In my experience, this arrangement has worked well to cut down on confused shouting and/or awkward pauses. If the space you have lends itself to different options for your students, feel free to get creative.

Step 5: Host the first meeting and reflect.

On the day of the initial video conference, make sure to reaffirm the time (and time zone) with the partner teacher. Also, check to see that the equipment works and you have a strong internet connection. Remind students to be respectful and open-minded. After the first meetup, invite students to share what they enjoyed most, and three things they learned during the conversation. Ask them for ideas on improving the next video conference.

Step 6: Exchange perspectives on a global issue in a second meetup.

Coordinate and plan the next video conference with the partner teacher. In the second meetup, students will exchange perspectives and share experiences about a global issue, such as education, preparing for future careers, healthcare, human rights, animal rights, or the environment. Decide the issue with the partner teacher in advance. Each class will prepare a short, ten-minutes-or-less presentation to inform the partner class about the local laws, policies, practices, and controversies regarding the global issue. Your class might want to prepare a virtual presentation with examples and resources to accompany the oral presentation.

The agenda for this exchange is simple. Say a quick greeting before the first class presents, followed by a questioning period. Then the next class presents, followed by a questioning period.

Students end by reflecting on how the new information has broadened their perspectives about the global issue.

Step 7: Elicit student feedback.

After the event, gather your students to share their thoughts and feelings on the meetups. Listen as they describe what they learned about their responsibilities as global citizens, communicating with people from different cultures, and how the exchanges broadened their perspectives on global issues.

OVERCOMING MISSION OBSTACLES

Setting up a successful global exchange presents certain challenges, such as finding an available partner within a time zone that works for both schools. Additionally, students need discussion and training on how to be culturally sensitive and communicate effectively and respectfully even when faced with different accents and forms of English. Here are strategies for meeting these challenges.

Where do I find partner classes? The Skype in the Classroom website has a spot to post your project and contact information for other classes to see. PenPal Schools, ePALS, and Skolinks are other websites that connect classes from different countries. You can also connect with teachers on your social networks. Twitter is a great resource. Tweet an invitation to the project and include the hashtags #ELTChat and #Langchat to specifically target international teachers. Facebook and Google Plus have groups and communities that teachers join to connect their classes globally. Conduct searches with these queries: global classrooms, Mystery Hangouts, or Skype educators.

How can I effectively collaborate with a teacher who is in a different time zone? Setting up a successful meetup requires both teachers to quickly and easily communicate across time zones. Determine which social networks and messaging apps you both already use so no one has to register for another platform. Many message apps on these social networks have features to easily plan projects, such as the ability to share links, post images and videos, leave voice messages, attach documents, and encourage each other with stickers and emojis.

How do I prepare my students to best communicate with non-native English speakers? Most speakers of English in the world are non-native speakers. English is their second or third language. Throughout their lives, our learners will need to communicate effectively while encountering foreign accents and different versions of English. Prepare your students by exposing them to video interviews or podcasts that include accents from the partner school's country. This will help them become familiar with the accent and increase understanding during the conversation.

Foremost, learners need to treat each other with respect and not show frustration, shout, rush others, or ask them to speak correct English. Instead, guide them to be patient and ask clarifying questions to slow down the conversation. It may be appropriate to point out that the partner school made the effort to communicate in English, and to imagine the difficulty of learning their language.

What if students want to continue communicating with each other? It's exciting to meet peers from a different country, and your students may want to continue the conversations. Instead of allowing students to contact each other privately, provide a safe environment for continued exchanges. Create a private virtual space for the classes to meet. Schoology and Edmodo are safe virtual learning environments where students can post questions and quickly respond to each other. These spaces are easy to manage and monitor. Make participation voluntary so you don't create extra work for yourself.

THE MISSION IN ACTION

Anthippi Harou teaches primary school in Athens, Greece. Every year her students take part in an eTwinning project on a safe platform, which encourages communication and collaboration in English between schools of different European countries. Anthippi conducted a school project with fifth-graders in 2015-16, entitled, "What is Life Like in Another Country?" The fifth-graders conducted Skype interviews with a class in Italy.

Both teachers were well prepared before the actual meeting. First, they exchanged messages about the content, date, time, and the process of the meeting. Then, they collaborated using an online Word document and Skyped each other to test their internet connections and discuss the content and process of the students' virtual meetings. Each school would ask the other ten questions about their country, and then answer the other school's questions. The limit was to ensure the Skype meeting would last for one teaching session (about fifty minutes). The teachers took into consideration the time spent on each school's answers.

After collaborating, both teachers encouraged their students to brainstorm questions to ask about the partner school. Each class decided on the ten most valuable questions from all the ideas, and the teachers exchanged the questions with each other. They encouraged students to prepare answers by taking notes and searching the web for details. Together they edited their answers and held a mock meeting before the actual meetup between the schools.

According to Anthippi, the preparation ensured that the actual Skype meeting was a great success. What follows is Anthippi's summary of the exciting experience.

> The Skype meeting provided us with the opportunity to open our classroom door to another classroom across Europe. We, in turn, entered and experienced another school's classroom that we would have never had the chance to visit in any other way. The students responded to their eTwinning partners and the teachers with great enthusiasm using English to communicate. In that special moment of our synchronous communication, the students realized they had actually been working with real people, i.e., their virtual friends in their project. Skyping with their partners confirmed that the students' work had indeed been shared with a true audience. The time went smoothly throughout the online meeting with lots of meaningful interaction and great joy reflected in the kids' big smiles!
>
> The students felt proud they were able to communicate their messages in a foreign language. They expressed their satisfaction by characterizing their Skype experience as an unforgettable one, and they enthusiastically spread the news both to their friends from other classrooms in our school and to their parents. They gained focused knowledge, which they were eager to acquire through the questions they had prepared; they practiced their English as a foreign language for a real purpose; and above all they

enjoyed the exhilarating experience. Finally, they ranked the Skype meeting as one of their top favourite activities in their eTwinning project evaluation.

Global exchanges expose learners to different cultures, perspectives, and ways of life. At first, these differences will seem strange and challenge students' ideals and beliefs. As the communication continues, the classes involved will find common interests, shared experiences, and core values to form bonds. Both classes will learn how to respect and celebrate different types of thinking, lifestyles, fashion, education, accents, religions, and beliefs. These are important traits our young, global citizens need to resolve conflicts and drive positive change in the world.

ENLIGHTEN THE WORLD AS A CITIZEN SCIENTIST

Conduct Real-World Field Research

[Science] is more than a school subject, or the periodic table, or the properties of waves. It is an approach to the world, a critical way to understand and explore and engage with the world, and then have the capacity to change that world.
— BARACK OBAMA, FORMER U.S. PRESIDENT

THE PROBLEM: EDUCATION FOCUSES ON ANSWERS INSTEAD OF UNDERSTANDING PROBLEMS

THE FIELD OF Science, Technology, Engineering, and Math (STEM) is at the heart of innovation, yet sadly, so few of our students pursue these areas because they don't see themselves as problem-solvers or innovators. Schools waste students' intelligence on solving textbook problems with only one possible answer. In real life, the problems that impact people and environments are complex and require our learners to spend time exploring them and approaching them in new ways. This is why we must engage kids in real-world research at the core of STEM; research that involves inquiry, observation, data collection, analysis, and experimentation. Investigative research takes the focus off finding one answer and encourages learners to gain intimate knowledge about a problem's complexities to innovate better approaches and strategies.

Our education system forces kids to provide answers instead of promoting field research. Providing answers kills the drive to intimately investigate a problem. However, field research transforms our learners into passionate investigators and inspires them to understand and fall in love with the subject. This is what leads to innovation, discovery, and invention.

THE MISSION: PUBLISH FIELD RESEARCH
TO ENLIGHTEN THE PUBLIC

It isn't enough to facilitate field research; students need to see their time and effort enhance people's understanding of the world. Citizen science achieves these objectives. Top innovators and intellectuals in the world teamed up with organizations like NASA and MIT to create toolkits, games, and apps to motivate individuals of any age to aid in critical research. These research projects advance science and cover other subject areas, including history, geography, and English.

By using their digital devices to conduct field research, students realize they carry powerful tools to transform themselves into scientists.

For this mission, our students act as local citizen scientists and use technology to conduct field research to advance the public's understanding (and their own!) of a complex problem or phenomenon. Students keep an observation journal to log their systematic investigation of a phenomenon, species, or ecosystem over a time period, and publish their research to make it available to the public as an interactive field guide.

MISSION PREP

Technology, especially mobile, is powerful for field research. Our young citizen scientists can use technology to snap pictures, take written notes, record audio commentary, enter data in spreadsheets, and film video of their observations. The following activities will help them develop important skills to conduct their field research.

- **Play I Spy with My Device.** Do you remember playing I Spy as a child? This activity is the digital version. Players use mobile devices or digital cameras to take pictures of objects they spy. First, review the topic you want your learners to observe, which might include bugs, plants, birds, or animals. Next, instruct learners to identify a real-world example and take a snapshot. Learners will show a zoomed-in version to peers, who try to guess what the object is and what it exemplifies in relation to the topic. For example, if the class is learning about geometric shapes, a student might take a snapshot of a bubble. Peers see the zoomed-in snapshot and guess that it's a bubble and represents a sphere. The purpose is to help your citizen scientists use their devices to take a closer look at their environments and record observations.

- **Annotate an image.** Citizen scientists use a mobile app to annotate a screenshot or photograph, maybe one they took during the I Spy with My Device activity. Note-taking and image-editing apps, like Evernote and Snapchat, feature tools to markup documents and images, such as highlighters, arrows, shapes, text boxes, and drawing tools. Instruct your learners to use these tools to analyze the subjects of their images and point out key observations. For example, if your students took pictures of plants, they could draw arrows to different parts accompanied by written labels. They might draw a circle around a raindrop on a leaf, and add text to say that it recently rained. Annotation is a key skill for digital literacy and research, and facilitates deeper analysis and understanding.

- **Contribute to a crowdsourced citizen science project.** Our digital learners can contribute to a multitude of citizen science projects spanning various subjects. Many of these projects require a small time commitment, likely the length of one class period. Researchers need our students' help to train computers to understand language, transcribe ancient papyri texts, map streams, spot light pollution, and identify looting at ancient sites. Find these projects and more at SciStarter.com. Students can share pictures they have taken of the plants, trees, birds, and animals in their area using an app such as Project Noah, Zydeco Inquiry, or BioKIDS.

MISSION LAUNCH

Step 1: Complete the Field Journal First Entry.

Your students will keep track of their daily observations in digital field journals for seven days. Feel free to shorten or extend the duration as needed. Use a digital tool of your choosing, but Google Docs, Evernote, and OneNote are good options. Students begin by completing the Field Journal First Entry (see Kit 18) in class with you. In this first entry, they briefly describe the subject, species, or phenomenon they will be observing. Assist students in narrowing down the subject by assigning a main topic or category, and to choose a subject they can easily observe for several days, so it should be near their homes or the school. Next, ask students to identify ways their research will benefit the community and the world. Under the "I wonder…" section, students generate five questions to guide their daily observations, and post an annotated photograph of their subject taken the same day.

Step 2: Conduct field research and document each day in the field journal.

The following day, your citizen scientists will bring in their field journals with the first entry completed, including their annotated photo. For the next six days, they take photos of their subject; document the date, time, and location; collect data in the form of measurements (optional); and take notes on what they see. They document the details in their Observation Log Entries (see Kit 19). Encourage your learners to use their "I wonder" questions to guide their observations, and to use the notes section to jot down any questions that arise. Now your citizen scientists are ready to continue their field observations. Give them a few days of wiggle room to complete their six observation log entries in their Field Journals.

Step 3 (optional): Gain insight from subject matter experts.

The best citizen science projects are a collaborative effort between official scientists, researchers, and the public. Ideally, you want to create an opportunity for students to show their field journals to a group of experts who can offer support and share their own experiences. You could contact a society of experts to virtually mentor or video conference with your students. If this isn't doable, schedule at least one physical or virtual meetup with a subject-matter expert. Plan a field trip to a local research lab, invite a guest expert to speak to the class, or plan a video conference. For more information on setting up a video conference, see Mission 7.

Step 4: Delineate Findings and Conclusions

When your citizen scientists complete their field research, they will reflect on the learning experience by filling out their Findings and Conclusions (see Kit 20). This last document guides them to review their initial five "I wonder" questions, and to share their findings, insights, and concluding thoughts.

Step 5: Transform observations into an interactive field guide.

Professional scientists and researchers publish their findings to provide people with greater understanding about the complexities of the world. Their findings are the stepping stones and inspiration to support other research projects that aim to answer big questions. Your citizen scientists will publish their findings in an interactive digital field guide to urge individuals to take a deeper look at their subjects and see them in a whole new light. (See Mission 4 for details about publishing a digital book.) Another option is to create a website with a page dedicated to each student's findings. Each page should include the most important insights from the field journal. Include the photographs from students' observation logs.

OVERCOMING MISSION OBSTACLES

Students are to conduct the majority of their field research on their own time. They (and their parents) might find this much autonomy challenging. The following strategies will help with any pushback or challenges.

What if students miss entries? Part of student autonomy is learning how to meet responsibilities and project deadlines. However, many of our learners are still developing these skills and may miss an entry due to scheduling conflicts, forgetfulness, bad weather, or illness. To help your citizen scientists keep on track, do daily quick checks of their progress. You don't need to collect or grade anything; just have students pull up their field journals as the class wraps up, and quickly scan their screens. Another tip is to give students a few weeks or a month to complete seven observations. This way, students have wiggle room and flexibility.

I don't teach a STEM subject. How do I adapt this mission for my subject? As noted in the mission description, "citizen science" research spans many subject areas. The idea is to facilitate systematic inquiry, observation, data analysis, and real-world learning. The topic doesn't have to specifically relate to your subject for students to achieve your curriculum standards. In addition to gaining essential digital research and literacy skills, students will learn how to generate questions, express ideas and thoughts in a digital journal, synthesize data from a variety of sources, and disseminate research into digital media for public consumption. If you prefer that students investigate a topic related to your subject, search for your subject matter on SciStarter. A list of citizen projects will provide you with ideas.

What safety precautions should my students follow during their field research? Your citizen scientists will be in the "field" and need to take safety precautions. As a class, come up with a list of safety tips and emergency procedures. Make sure students are dressed appropriately for any outdoor field research, and have an adult nearby. If they have allergies, they need to carry any medications they might need. Remind them to be aware of their surroundings. Also remind students to be respectful of nature and the subjects they are researching.

Do students have to conduct research outdoors? The simple answer is no. Many zoos, aquariums, and museums have webcams of animals, weather systems, national parks, the sky, major cities, historic sites, and traffic – and list them on the EarthCam website. These are great subjects for field journals.

THE MISSION IN ACTION

To help inform locals and visitors of Northwest Florida's hidden natural treasures, Andrea Santilli and her seventh-graders at Woodlawn Beach Middle School created the free interactive field guide, *Creatures, Plants and More! A Kid's Guide to Northwest Florida*, available to the public on the Apple iBooks store. The interactive field guide features stories, animated photos, and videos collected and compiled by Andrea's Advanced Life Science students.

Andrea collected research, images, and video from sixty-nine students, and had them apply this research to help educate others about their community's natural treasures. The students encouraged people from around the world to discover and experience Northwest Florida. iBooks recognizes the interactive field guide as a top download, with over 18,300 downloads from more than forty countries.

In addition to providing readers with a wealth of information, the field guide suggests that readers visit locations in Northwest Florida for themselves. The book makes it easy by providing links to each site. At the end of the book, two students appear in a short video to encourage readers to explore ten local areas: Gulf Islands National Seashore, Pensacola Beach and Fishing Pier, The Butterfly House, Blackwater River State Park, Fort Pickens State Park, Florida State Parks, Northwest Florida Trails, Pensacola, Navarre, and Gulf Breeze. Many of these organizations depend on visitors and tourists to keep their funding and existence. They are important to the area as educational resources and as protective advocates for ecosystems, creatures, and flora.

Teachers used the interactive field guide to assess student knowledge and help the middle school students understand practical applications and the "real-world" impact of the units they learned in school. To kickstart work on the guide, Andrea took the class on a field trip to give students the opportunity to take pictures of their organisms. The students conducted research using their books, notes, and the internet. Andrea provided .edu, .org, and scientific magazine websites for them to explore.

Andrea describes the most exciting part of the project for her and the students:

> The most exciting part for the kids was that they were published and got recognition for their work via newspapers, TV, etc. The most exciting part for me was that they could now see the true value of learning about science, how it applied to the real world, how my most difficult students became "experts" in the field and had tremendous learning gains due to this whole experience.

Technology enables our students to contribute research and knowledge to real scientific discoveries and advancements that improve the world. By using their digital devices to conduct field research, students realize they carry powerful tools to transform themselves into scientists. When students realize the impact their research makes on their community and the world, they feel more empowered to pursue expertise in STEM. Field research opens our citizen scientists to the learning potential in all that surrounds them, and sparks curiosity, encourages exploration, and drives wonder.

MISSION 9

APPRECIATE OTHERS WITH A DIGITAL BADGE

Recognize Values, Not Just Grades

Celebrate what you want to see more of.
— THOMAS J. PETERS, AMERICAN AUTHOR

THE PROBLEM: GRADES DON'T RECOGNIZE THE MOST IMPORTANT SKILLS

RECOGNITION AND APPRECIATION are an integral part of our work, communities, government, sports, education, and extracurricular activities. Other organizations do a much better job recognizing skills, great acts, talent, and diligence than schools do. They give their members pins, patches, and insignias to recognize achievements, and recipients wear the badges with pride.

One of the most familiar examples is the military. Military men and women have badges and pins on their uniforms to display their rank and honors. Other members of the military see these insignias on the uniform and know how to address and salute the soldiers. The members know what the soldier has accomplished to earn these insignias. Girl Scouts and Boy Scouts give patches for members to wear when they learn a new skill or help someone. Martial arts teams give different color belts to show ranking and achievement. Sports teams give players patches for winning, attending tournaments, or achieving awards.

Schools focus on grades, but grades fail to show potential employers the skills students possess that make them good team players, project leaders, presenters, innovators, problem solvers, and so forth. Because schools use grades and test scores as the main measurements of success, students spend less time focusing on the non-graded qualities of citizenship, leadership skills, and achievements. We need to go beyond recognizing the basic achievement of knowledge and find ways to appreciate skills, talents, and accomplishments.

THE MISSION: RECOGNIZE ACHIEVEMENTS WITH DIGITAL BADGES

Just as patches and pins demonstrate achievement in various organizations, students can award digital badges to recognize other students for their accomplishments. A digital badge is a micro-credential given through a digital platform after an authority validates that the receiver earned the achievement, skill, or quality. Various web tools simplify designing, issuing, and displaying digital badges. Badging platforms display these micro-credentials on a web page along with the details showing why the student earned the badges. Students can continue earning their digital badges throughout their education journey. When they apply for scholarships, special programs, magnet schools, internships, colleges, or job positions, their digital badge portfolios can illustrate the skills and qualities they possess.

When students issue their badges, they send a message to their peers that they recognize their achievements and skills.

For this mission, students get started by designing digital badges to issue to their peers. The process includes students defining the criteria to earn the badge, understanding how to provide evidence to support earning a badge (usually a link to the completed task), and offering validation or testimony of the student's achievement.

MISSION PREP

Before students begin designing their own badges, they need a basic understanding of the concept and purpose of digital badging. The following activities provide learners with this foundation:

- **Create a table to display achievement insignias.**
  Inspire students to make a real-world connection to the concept of digital badging. Start by helping them reflect on the ways that organizations, clubs, or games have recognized achievements and skills.

See the Mission Toolkit (Kit 21) for the Table of Achievements Received handout, a three-column table that students can complete with this information. In the first column, students list their achievements. They can list fictional achievements if they prefer. In the second column, students draw or post an image of the emblem, award, or insignia. In the third column, students name the organization that recognized their achievements.

- **Evaluate digital badges.** Show students examples of digital badges issued on different platforms. Students choose three badges they like and complete a table. An example of a completed table is available in the Mission Toolkit (Kit 22) with the following information: the badge name, an image of the badge, the criteria, and a criteria example. Find great examples of badges designed for K-12 on Makewaves and on the Corona-Norco Unified School District: Passport to Success website.

- **Earn badges.** Your learners have opportunities to earn digital badges for completing challenges to make them better digital citizens or more adept at navigating the internet. OpenBadges has a series of web-smart challenges for students to earn the Super Girl and the Navigator badge. The challenges are appropriate for middle school and high school students to complete. Visit the Common Sense Media Organization to see a set of badges for teachers to issue to their K-12 students who complete their digital citizenship units.

- **Determine what to recognize with digital badges.** In small groups, students discuss actions and skills to recognize with digital badges. Each group should come up with at least ten actions, achievements, or skills. They might consider the following ideas: a "wow" idea, a thoughtful question, helping peers, offering tech support, an exceptional presentation, being a team player, leadership, creative design, digital citizenship, an interesting share, a cool discovery, taught me something new today, a great blog post, or a thoughtful comment. Gather all the lists and come up with a class-approved list. Help students cross off normal expectations, such as attending class, showing up on time, or turning in work. Badges highlight performance that goes above and beyond.

MISSION LAUNCH

Step 1: Use the template to envision the badge.

Hand students the Badge Design Template provided in the Mission Toolkit (see Kit 23) to plan the criteria, evidence, and look of their digital badges. Students choose a skill or achievement from the class-approved list, determine the criteria, and list simple steps for earning the badge. They briefly describe the required evidence and acceptable forms of evidence, such as a URL, image, or written description.

Step 2: Design the digital badge.

Students draw badge designs, and transform their drawings into digital tokens. They may want to use graphic design web tools such as Google Drawings, Canva, Makebadges, Open Badges, or ClassBadges to create the image of their badges and download them as PNGs or JPGs. Be sure they properly name each image file with the badge name and the student's name. Students submit the digital badge image file and the Badge Design Template to you for feedback and approval.

Step 3: Create a form for peers to earn the badge.

Approve the students' designs, criteria, and evidence. Now, based on the information in the Badge Design Template, they create forms for their peers to submit evidence to earn the digital badges. Kit 24 in the Mission Toolkit illustrates a student form for earning a Gem Comment Badge. The potential earner sees the badge name, the badge image, the criteria, and evidence requirements. I recommend Google Forms for students to complete this step. Learn more about creating Google Forms in *Hacking Google for Education*, which provides strategies for teachers, principals, and district administrators.

Step 4: Display and present the badges.

Upload all the digital badge images to a website. Link images to the submission forms created in Step 3. When students click on the digital badge they want to earn, the submission form should appear. When the website is ready to go with all the badges, have students share quick presentations to their peers, displaying the digital badges they designed, along with the criteria and evidence guidelines.

Step 5: Generate excitement about earning their peers' badges.

Encourage students to earn as many digital badges as they would like, and set a minimum requirement for the quantity they must earn by the end of the month or semester. If you wish, allow students to nominate their peers to earn badges. To nominate a peer, the student completes the same submission form and notes that the entry is a nomination.

Step 6: Reinforce guidelines for issuing badges.

Before issuing their digital badges, students must review the evidence and speak with peers to ensure they meet all the criteria. If a student doesn't feel the peer has met the criteria, the student should let the peer know what else they must do to earn the badge. Every student should have the opportunity to attempt to earn any badge and to reapply for it multiple times until he fulfills the requirements. When the student decides to issue a badge, she should include a testimonial about the peer receiving the badge.

Step 7: Display and share the digital badges.

Students display the badges they receive on a digital badge platform, a digital portfolio, or website. Encourage students to also share their badges on their blogs or social media networks so others can celebrate their achievements with them. Another way to create excitement for earning digital badges is by displaying a chart with all the students' names and the badges they earned. Create this chart on posterboard or on the class website.

OVERCOMING MISSION OBSTACLES

Although many case studies demonstrate the positive impact of digital badges on learning, only a few schools and districts have an official digital badging program. Digital badging is a new trend for K-12 schools and many misconceptions exist. Here are solutions to obstacles you might encounter.

What if parents and students feel digital badging is another gimmick? Digital badging is often tied to gamification, which makes some parents, students, and teachers skeptical about the value. However, if teachers implement digital badges properly, it will motivate and empower their learners. Grades and test scores are the main ways schools evaluate students, but they do not represent to colleges, internships, or employers the most important skills and traits that students possess. They also don't reveal leadership, teamwork, creativity, and other soft skills. Therefore, digital badges serve an important purpose in education by providing a broader picture of student achievements and skills.

This portfolio of badges can accompany student report cards to display achievements and skills. Moreover, students and parents can click on the badges to see the attached criteria, evidence, and testimony. The evidence illustrates the effort that went into meeting the requirements for earning the badges.

How do I ensure badges tap into extrinsic motivation? The activities in the Mission Prep section are essential for helping students understand the concept and purpose of digital badges. We need to make sure students design digital badges to recognize achievements, skills, and heroic acts. Guide them to avoid designing digital badges that recognize normal requirements and expectations, such as showing up to class on time, keeping their desks clean, completing homework, or making a high score.

How do I prevent students from over-issuing badges to their friends? It's tempting for students to generously issue digital badges to their friends or attempt to earn badges designed by their friends. Monitor the situation, and remind students that their teachers, future employers, volunteer program coordinators, and colleges may evaluate the badges as credentials. These entities will provide students with opportunities based on skills and qualities; therefore, it is in students' best interests to earn badges that recognize their individual achievements, skills, and traits. Additionally, students provide testimonials for peers who earn their badges, and these testimonials mean they are vouching for their peers. Make sure to give students time to submit and evaluate the evidence for earning their badges.

Isn't digital badging more valid if students use a digital badging platform? This mission introduces you and your students to the concept of digital badging. We designed these steps so you and your students aren't required to sign up and register for one digital badging platform. If you decide to implement digital badges into your curriculum, choose a digital badging platform designed for education, such as Makewaves, Credly, Mozilla Backpack, Badgelist, and ClassBadges. These platforms require issuers and receivers to register for an account.

THE MISSION IN ACTION

For years, I have issued digital badges to motivate my learners to complete extra learning missions and celebrate their peers' achievements. One day, I decided to take a risk and ask a group of learners to design their own digital badges and issue them to peers. We were using Cred.ly to issue and display our badges so students continued to use this badging platform to design their own, host them, and issue them.

This opportunity excited students, who quickly designed their badges and posted them with a description and a link to earn them on our virtual classroom. Their peers could click the link, view the criteria, and submit evidence to attempt to earn the badge. The students' ideas astonished me. They designed badges to recognize when peers showed excellence in their work, shared a useful tip, answered a difficult question with useful information, played a certain amount of learning games, and helped other peers with their work.

Getting students to design and issue digital badges was an experiment and I was nervous about the outcome. However, the students surprised me in many ways. They did not quickly issue their badges to friends as I feared. Instead, students were cautious when awarding their badges and carefully went through past posts and activities to select who should achieve their digital badges based on the criteria. In some cases, the student who designed the badge asked questions of those to whom they considered awarding a badge. The questions were about a particular post or activity to better determine if that student should earn the badge.

This project motivated students, who were excited to share their badges with everyone. They posted the badges on Twitter and other social networks so that those outside the class could celebrate their achievements. Another positive result was that our group became a community. Students appreciated being recognized by their peers and felt good about issuing badges to recognize the skills and traits of others.

Digital badging helps students reflect on citizenship and builds character. Designing the badges helps them determine what they value in others, and builds positive relationships within the class. When students issue their badges, they send a message to their peers that they recognize their achievements and skills. These are the building blocks of transforming a class into a community. Digital badging is the way to celebrate the strengths of all students and make them feel they are much more than a score or letter grade.

MISSION 10

CROWDFUND INNOVATION TO FIND SOLUTIONS

Engage Social Media to Fundraise for a Cause

*Never doubt that a small group of thoughtful, committed citizens can change the world. Indeed,
it is the only thing that ever has.*
– MARGARET MEAD, AMERICAN CULTURAL ANTHROPOLOGIST / AUTHOR

THE PROBLEM: SCHOOLS DON'T HELP KIDS INNOVATE SOLUTIONS TO MAKE A DIFFERENCE

MANY STUDENTS I have interviewed during my travels to more than twenty countries do great things outside the classroom. I met a thirteen-year-old who began running her charity for children in Uganda at the age of six. I interviewed an eight-year-old boy who has helped feed millions of homeless people, and a sixteen-year-old who invented a method for detecting pancreatic cancer at early stages.

Unfortunately, many of these young innovators expressed how teachers and principals threatened to fail them versus help them succeed. Teachers told them that their innovations weren't part of the school curriculum. Clearly, schools need to do better. We need to find ways to tap into students' passions, support their innovations, and tie these pursuits into learning math, science, history, or literacy. School policy is so hung up on standardized testing results and achieving rigid curriculum goals that we miss teaching students to be modern innovators who solve real-world problems.

THE MISSION: CROWDFUND INNOVATION

Our kids want to improve their communities and make a difference in the world. Our projects and curriculum may help students innovate solutions to problems, but we have to push this further. Students need to know how modern innovators use the internet to pitch ideas, fundraise, and implement their solutions. Crowdfunding is the current way innovators and entrepreneurs build community support and fund their projects. It involves setting up a fundraising website, designing a campaign to compel others to donate, sharing the campaign with a large audience, accepting donations, and using those donations to carry out projects to fruition. In this mission, students will identify and investigate a local need, devise ways to improve the situation, and design a class crowdfunding campaign to implement the ideas and make an impact on their communities.

  Students learn how to create a pitch that appeals to an audience and motivates them to invest in the ideas and innovation.

MISSION PREP

Let's teach students how to use the internet to be successful innovators and gain support for their innovations. The following activities introduce learners to the power of crowdfunding:

- **Introduce students to young entrepreneurs.** When other young people use social media and technology to innovate or make a meaningful difference, it inspires our students. Together, analyze the crowdfunding campaigns led by young innovators. TED has created a playlist – Talks by Brilliant Kids and Teens – of video-recorded TED Talks by kids and teens. Newsela has a collection of articles with the stories of young inventors, called Kid Innovators, with quizzes and writing activities.

- **Evaluate crowdfunding campaigns created by other classes.** The crowdfunding platforms specifically designed for teachers and students include DonorsChoose, PledgeCents, ClassWish, AdoptAClassroom, and Digital Wish. Students evaluate one of the campaigns using the set of reflection questions provided in the Mission Toolkit (see Kit 25).

- **Identify a local need and crowdsource knowledge about the need.** As a class, brainstorm a list of local problems and needs. Create a poll for students to vote on the top issue they are interested in investigating, and share the results with the class. Give students time to discover three facts about each need. Design a collaborative class Google Document or Padlet for all the students to list their three facts. This document will provide insight to the class.

- **Develop ideas to improve the situation.** Direct students to jot down ideas to the question, "If the class raised $500, how could we improve the situation?" Collect these ideas and place them in a poll for a class vote. The crowdfunding campaign will support the winning idea.

MISSION LAUNCH

Step 1: Brainstorm the look and details of the campaign page.

Register for a crowdfunding platform to host the class campaign. You should be the only administrator of the account. Divide students into small groups to collaborate on the campaign page design. Introduce the platform to the groups and show them the required sections to complete. Depending on the platform, these sections might include a name for the campaign, the project description, the goal amount, an image, and the breakdown of the fund allocation.

Step 2: Pitch and vote on a design.

Provide the groups with tips on designing successful crowd-funding campaigns; you can find ideas on the platform you choose. You may want to download Edutopia's free PDF guide, *Raise Money for Your School Using Crowdfunding* – full of great tips to create successful campaigns. Another great resource is the article, "Raise Money With Crowdfunding: Top 9 Tips for Schools," created by Education World. These resources provide students with help crafting a campaign story and using social media to attract donors. The groups collaborate on the page details and pitch their ideas to the class, which votes on the best parts of each pitch to consider for the final design. The final design will incorporate ideas from each pitch.

Step 3: Create graphics to announce the campaign on social media.

The most successful crowdfunding campaigns are shared on social media. DonorsChoose provides free graphics to accompany social media posts, which you can find under the section, Shareable Images to Spread the Word About Your Project. Each student creates a compelling visual to use when they are ready to announce to friends, family, and their community on social media that they are raising donations for a crowdfunding campaign. Students can use any image-editing software, program, or web tool (such as Canva and EduBuncee) to create their visuals.

Step 4: Produce a video to announce the campaign.

Many platforms report that crowdfunding campaigns with professionally made videos raise more funds than those without. The recommended video length is one to three minutes. Students will have fun producing a short animated video illustrating how the campaign will improve the situation. They may want to use video-creation tools such as Biteable, PowToon, or MySimpleShow.

Step 5: Spread the word on social media.

Now it's time for students to share the campaign on social media. Students will create a buzz and attract donors by sharing the visuals and videos on their social networks.

Step 6: Keep the momentum going!

Decide the timeframe of the crowdfunding campaign. Most campaigns run thirty to ninety days. It is important that students continue to promote the campaign until they meet the funding goals. Divide the total amount of days by the number of students and assign students to be in charge of the campaign's social media management for a set number of days. Create a calendar and post these dates and responsibilities. Students will be in charge of posting updates on social networks, maintaining the crowdfunding page, updating donors, and checking the analytics and progress. Rotating students keeps the campaign fresh. Each student will be able to contribute fresh ideas, energy, and share the news with different audiences.

Step 7: Share the impact to the community.

After students complete the crowdfunded campaign, spend time together reflecting on the impact, and how they can document the outcomes. One idea is to create a digital slideshow with highlights of the campaign and how it helped the community. Encourage them to include visuals, quotes from students involved, and testimonies from the people impacted. They may want to include a slide to thank everyone who donated and supported the campaign.

OVERCOMING MISSION OBSTACLES

Crowdfunding is the digital way to fundraise, and it's an important skillset for our young innovators to gain. An exchange of money takes place, which means schools and teachers are responsible for ensuring they use the funds ethically. Moreover, teachers need to thank parents, the community, school staff, and students for their efforts, and share an update with them. The following tips will help ensure the crowdfunding campaign is successful.

How do I convince leadership to support this project? Get approval from leadership to ensure you follow the school's fundraising policies and so that your project is tax-exempt. Present the project to your leadership, outline learning objectives that students will achieve, and highlight additional benefits of crowdfunding, such as bringing good press to the school and meeting a local need. Most leadership will support an enthusiastic teacher and passionate students wanting to make a difference.

Be sure to check out the free materials the crowdfunding platforms provide to teachers to help them inform school leadership and parents. In the Help sections of the crowdfunding websites, you will find flyers, promotional materials, and videos explaining the process and benefits. Show your school leadership examples of similar well-designed campaigns on the platform.

Is the project part of the curriculum? Your curriculum must be tied to the class campaign that benefits a community need, especially if you want school leadership and parents to support it. Crowdsourcing campaigns take an investment of time, and to justify the time, parents and school administration want to make sure the campaign is covering content related to your subject material or helping students learn in some way. To find a topic aligned with curriculum objectives, conduct a search on various crowdfunding platforms to see what other teachers in your subject area have done. Teachers have created campaigns to purchase classroom supplies, buy a 3D printer, create a maker space, buy equipment for a school club, raise funds for a national contest, or set up a summer camp.

How do I ensure the class reaches the funding goals? Design this initial campaign to improve a situation by starting with an achievable goal. For example, if the class needs a set of iPads, aim to raise funds to create an iPad station this year. You can continue the campaign with the next class, but make sure your students understand they are the first part of a longer plan. Also, note that some crowdfunding platforms penalize campaigns that don't receive enough donations. When designing a campaign, make sure the platform allows you to keep any funds raised even if the campaign doesn't reach its goal.

How do I keep the momentum going when we have other material to cover? Most crowdfunding campaigns require a month or more to be successful, in addition to the time it takes to introduce the idea of crowdfunding, and time for students to design their campaigns. You won't need a lot of class time to manage the campaign, so don't stress about that. Each student needs to take charge so this is student-driven versus teacher-driven. Assign each student to be in charge of the campaign for a set amount of days. They manage the campaign during their free time. This ensures every student develops his or her project management skills and takes on a leadership role.

THE MISSION IN ACTION

Colleen Rose is teacher and technology champion at Nipigon-Red Rock District High School in Canada. Colleen had students in her Equity, Diversity, and Social Justice class research the problem of Canada's high grocery prices and how these prices relate to social justice. Students watched the video, *The High Price of Basic Groceries in Canada's North*. They reviewed statistical data and also read the article, "When $500 Isn't Enough to Buy Groceries for a Week," posted on the Chatelaine's website.

To further understand the problem, students worked in small groups and prepared a week's worth of meal plans and grocery lists for a family of four. They created a mind map with the topic header, *What do we do with our knowledge of food security?* These mind maps inspired one student group to create a GoFundMe crowdfunding campaign to raise funds and awareness for the Niqinik Nuatsivik Food Bank in Iqaluit. The group created the GoFundMe page at the beginning of November 2016 and it ran for a month. The goal was $2,000, but donations totaled $180 by the deadline. GoFundMe is one crowdfunding platform that takes a percentage of funds raised, so students were only given $163.38; however, the campaign inspired the local Rotary Club to donate an additional $480 to the students' cause.

This project was a moving experience for other students, who wanted to create awareness videos about raising funds to feed local families. One video, *Help Canada's North*, features interviews with students expressing their disappointment and sadness for the situation. An interviewer asked students how they would feel if they were unable to feed their families, and many said they would feel overwhelmed. They asked what students could do to help, and they expressed the need to donate funds to the food bank and bring awareness to the situation.

Leaders of nonprofits that help feed Canadians – including representatives from Arctic Co-operatives Ltd., Feeding Nunavut, and the Iqaluit Food Bank – saw the video. They answered students' questions about the situation and congratulated them on raising awareness and funds for a local food bank. The call highlighted how solely donating food is not as helpful as bringing awareness and raising funds. The student campaign fed four families, and the students were thrilled that they were able to make a meaningful impact for Canadians. They gathered more information about the problem and spoke with community leaders on how to move forward with their knowledge. Colleen Rose reflects that the project shows how important it is for educators to reach beyond the classroom and inspire students to make an impact on the world around them.

Technology and social media provide our students with the power to meaningfully impact their communities with their learning, and schools can support and facilitate students in their efforts to make a difference in the world. This learning mission helps students gain experience designing compelling fundraising campaigns using technology and social media to share the stories behind their fundraising. Students learn how to create a pitch that appeals to an audience and motivates them to invest in the ideas and innovation. By supporting such a mission, teachers and schools become part of the journey toward inspiring students to go beyond basic problem solving to implementing solutions.

CONCLUSION

MEANINGFUL LEARNING MISSIONS
MAKE A POWERFUL IMPACT

SOCIAL MEDIA HAS introduced me to incredible teachers around the world and allowed me to travel to their schools and work with their learners. One connection led me to Slovenia where the teachers wanted to see mission-based learning in action with their teens. We gathered more than eighty students in one large room. The teachers introduced me and announced to the high schoolers that they would work in small groups and use their devices to carry out a task with me. Excitement was in the air. I showed them slides introducing them to the mission. I started with a scenario: the XYZ Company wanted to make the next great app for teens and needed their help to identify their major problems and develop an app to solve one. They would introduce their app ideas in a short video, no longer than a minute.

I provided students with five minutes to brainstorm, five

minutes to learn their roles and responsibilities, and twenty minutes to film, edit, and produce their videos. The team of teachers and I walked around and facilitated. We played the videos, and the app inventions were amazing! They included a Jackie Chan app to ward off bullies, a transporter app to get to school on time, and an app to help students quit smoking. Before the lesson, the teachers expressed their reservations. They believed students would access their social networks or act inappropriately. Instead, their students surprised them by staying focused and working well together to come up with innovative ideas. The teachers hadn't seen them so enthusiastic about learning, and they were eager to see what students could create by accomplishing more missions with their devices.

A thousand years ago, knowledge and the ability to innovate belonged to the elite, and the majority of non-elite accepted their stations in life. In our modern world, the internet has helped to change this dynamic. Our students live at an incredible time when anyone, anywhere, has access to experts, creativity tools, and a global audience to make a difference in the world. Unfortunately, many use the tools to cause pain and suffering.

Educators can make a difference. Our responsibilities have changed with the advent of web tools, applications, and social media. We must challenge our students to achieve great things with technology and to develop the world they envision. Each of the ten missions in this book empowers students to make a meaningful impact on their communities using their skills, knowledge, peers, and the amazing technology at their fingertips. The missions introduce students to the roles they play as digital citizens and challenge them to carry out those roles ethically and mindfully. As they accomplish these missions, your learners will tap into their inner heroes and explorers. They will reflect on their digital identities, strengthen those identities, and innovate with technology to improve their communities and the world.

MISSION TOOLKIT

KIT 1:

STORYBOARD FOR A
GAME WALKTHROUGH

Download available at ShellyTerrell.com/EdTechMissions

Game Scene   Instructions

KIT 2:
THE FIRST SELFIE INQUIRY QUESTIONS

1. How many times do you think Cornelius took this selfie?

2. What makes this selfie interesting?

3. What would you improve about this selfie?

4. Why do you think Cornelius took this selfie?

5. What do you notice about Cornelius' stance, facial expression, clothing, hair style, and emotions?

6. What do you think these choices say about Cornelius as a person and about his emotions captured in this selfie?

7. What do you think Cornelius would say about selfies today?

KIT 3:

AROUND THE WORLD IN 360 DEGREES INQUIRY QUESTIONS

1. Which of Alex Chacon's selfies were your favorites? Why?

2. What is different about Alex Chacon's selfies vs. selfies taken by you or your peers?

3. Describe at least two different experiences Alex Chacon had or places he visited based on his selfies.

4. What makes Alex Chacon's selfies meaningful?

5. Have you ever met someone of a different religion, ethnicity, or from a different country? Describe your experience.

6. List personality traits and characteristics you believe Alex Chacon possesses based on his selfie adventure.

7. How do you think Alex Chacon was able to convince people who spoke a different language or who were strangers to participate in his selfie adventure?

KIT 4:

FISM NETWORK TEMPLATE

Download available at ShellyTerrell.com/EdTechMissions

Born on

FISM

☆

☆

☆

☆

☆

☆

KIT 4

CONTINUED: FISM NETWORK MESSAGING TEMPLATES

Download available at ShellyTerrell.com/EdTechMissions

FISM

KIT 5:
DIGITAL TRAILS DISCUSSION PROMPTS
Download available at ShellyTerrell.com/EdTechMissions

- What is your favorite social network and why?

- Have you ever been bullied online?

- Would you stick up for a friend who is being bullied online? How?

- Do you think people can get addicted to being on the internet?

- How do you think the internet and technology impact your relationships with your peers?

- How do you think the internet and technology impact your relationships with your family?

- Can you spend too much time online? How does this negatively impact your life?

- Did you ever post something private then later regret it?

- Have you ever been mean to anyone online? Did you feel badly about it?

- Do you think selfies are silly or cool? Why?

- How many social networks do you belong to?

- How much time do you spend on the internet?

- What do you do most of the time when you are online?

- Do you message or text others?

- Do you ever curse online?

- Do you care about grammar or spelling in your posts or the posts of others?

- Have you ever saved an image or taken a screen-shot of what others posted online?

- How would you feel if a company used an image you posted online to make a lot of money, and didn't ask your permission?

- Have you ever interacted with someone online who you haven't met in person?

- Do you accept friends or followers who you've never met personally?

- Has a person you have never met ever made you feel uncomfortable online?

- Do you check the profile of every person you "friend?"

- Do you tend to trust most people online?

- How would you feel if someone shared your private gossip publicly?

- What do you do online that you would never do in person?

- Why is protecting your privacy important?

- What would you do if your friends posted a picture of you that you didn't like?

- Do you publicly share your relationship status with people online?

- When a friendship or relationship ends do you erase the digital footprint of it?

- What do you usually share on your social networks?

- If someone is mean to you online, do you think it is okay to retaliate?

- What things annoy you about social media?

- Do you think your private thoughts or secrets are safe to share online?

KIT 6:
DIGITAL FOOTPRINT INVESTIGATION
Download available at ShellyTerrell.com/EdTechMissions

	Social Network: (e.g,. Instagram)	Social Network:
Number of Friends or followers		
Top post (describe it)		
Was it a public or private post?		
How many people "liked" and "shared" it?		
What personal information was included in the post?		
How many days, weeks, or years has this been posted?		
Most popular personal photo or media shared (describe it)		
Was it public or private?		
How many people "liked" and "shared" it?		
What type of comments did you receive?		
What personal information was included in the image?		
How many days, weeks, or years has this been posted?		

KIT 7:

HISTORICAL FIGURE TRAITS MAP

Download available at ShellyTerrell.com/EdTechMissions

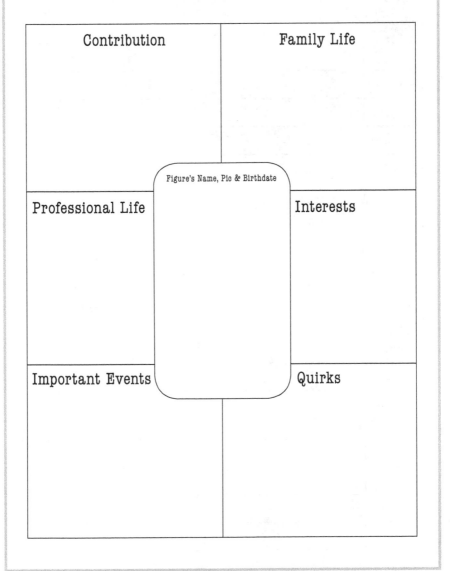

Contribution

Family Life

Professional Life

Figure's Name, Pic & Birthdate

Interests

Important Events

Quirks

KIT 8:
HANDOUT OF LICENSING INFORMATION
Download available at ShellyTerrell.com/EdTechMissions

Image	
url	
license	
restrictions	
attribution	

Gif	
url	
license	
restrictions	
attribution	

Audio	
url	
license	
restrictions	
attribution	

Video	
url	
license	
restrictions	
attribution	

KIT 9:

CHAPTER LAYOUT SAMPLES
FOR DIGITAL BOOK

Download Available at ShellyTerrell.com/EdTechMissions

Title

By Student Name

Key learning points

- Point 1
- Point 2
- Point 3
- Point 4

Insert media

Caption linked to the source with appropriate attribution

Insert text or media

Insert text

Interactive activity

CHAPTER LAYOUT SAMPLES FOR DIGITAL BOOK - CONTINUED

Title

By Student Name

Insert text or media

Interactive activity

Insert text or media

References

KIT 10:
DEBATE THE ISSUES POLL QUESTIONS

- Do you get offended when others disagree with you?

- Do you think listening to opposite views benefits you?

- Do you tend to "friend" people who mostly agree with you?

- Do you have close friends who have religious beliefs different than yours?

- Do you have close friends who share a different culture than you?

- Do you have close friends with a different economic status than you?

- Have you ever argued with anyone online?

- Do you enjoy online debates or avoid them?

KIT 11:

FINAL POST TEMPLATE

Download available at ShellyTerrell.com/EdTechMissions

I. Quote #1 by Peer's Name:

What I learned...

II. Quote #2 by Peer's Name:

What I learned...

III. Quote #3 by Peer's Name:

What I learned...

IV. Changes to my initial claim:

KIT 12:

TRACE THE SOURCE

Describe the content you shared:

Social network where it appeared:

Questions for investigation:

- What motivated you to reshare or "like" this content?

- How did the content appear on your feed? Who shared it from your network?

- Who is the creator or author of this content?

- Why did this person create this content?

- Did anyone from your network reshare or "like" this content?

- How many people?

- How many people "liked" or reshared the content from the person who brought it to your attention?

Reflection: What did you learn about the way information is spread on social networks and the part you play?

KIT 13:

EVALUATION FORM FOR A NEWS BROADCAST

News clip source:

Station/location:

Clip date:

Newscaster's name and background information:

What is the news event?

How does the reporter introduce this news?

How does the reporter set the mood and convey the tone of the news?

How does the reporter's voice change (pitch, speed, emphasis, volume, etc.) and what is the effect?

How does the reporter conclude the segment?

Describe any sound effects, background noise, or music you hear.

KIT 14:

NEWSCAST TEAM PLANNING

Download available at ShellyTerrell.com/EdTechMissions

News topic-

Team members and roles:

Interviewer:

Anchor:

Camera person:

Director/editor:

Details of your news story. These should be covered in the interviews:

Who?

What?

Where?

When?

Why?

Who will be interviewed and by which team member(s)?

What questions will be asked?

When will these interviews be recorded?

Which team member will record the interviews?

Describe the backdrop of each interview. Will you film at a location or use a green screen?

Describe any props or costumes needed and which team member is responsible for getting them.

KIT 15:

INTERVIEW REQUEST EMAIL TEMPLATE

Download available at ShellyTerrell.com/EdTechMissions

Dear Source's Name,

I am a/an (grade level) student at (school name). I would be honored to interview you about (topic) for my (class name) class. I found you through (list website or where you found them) when researching my topic. I enjoyed your (name an accomplishment, bog post, research, etc. you discovered) and would like to learn more from you. The interview should take about (time frame) via (name the media you will record the interview). The interview will be recorded and presented to (list audience– e.g., my peers, on my blog (provide link), or website).

I am available (list times). I understand if you are too busy and would be happy to talk with another colleague you could recommend with knowledge about this topic.

Thank you for your time. Feel free to reach me at (email address) or my teacher, (teacher's name), at (email address/phone number).

Sincerely,

Name
School Name
Class Name
Teacher's Name
Class Website or Student Blog

KIT 16:

EXAMPLE NEWSCAST AND SCRIPT

Download available at ShellyTerrell.com/EdTechMissions

Scene	Scene Description	Production Details	Script
Intro	Anchors, Sue and Jack, introduce the news story	*Backdrop*: News desk	Welcome to AZ News! I am Sue and I am Jack. Sue: Jack did you hear about the panda giving birth at the city zoo? Jack: Yes! This is the first panda to give birth there. Laura is live with the zookeeper to give us more exciting details.
1	Insert Laura's 30 second interview recording with the zookeeper.	*Backdrop*: In front of the panda exhigit at the zoo. Camera shot of the pandas	Prerecorded
2	Back to anchors, Sue and Jack	*Backdrop*: News desk	Sue: Jack that was one cute panda. Have you been to the zoo to see the baby panda? Jack: Not yet, but John is live with one excited kid who has seen the baby panda.
3	Insert John's 30 second interview with his younger brother who saw the panda.	*Backdrop*: At John's house. His brother is holding a stuffed panda.	Prerecorded
Closing	Anchors, Sue and Jack, end the newscast	*Backdrop*: News desk	Jack: That kid's excitement makes me want to go visit the baby panda. Sue, when do you plan on going? Sue: Special viewings of the baby panda are from 12 to 3pm Monday through Sunday. I will probably go this weekend. Jack: Maybe I will see you there! Maybe our viewers will see you there, too. Sue: I hope so! Well that's ournews for today. Thank you for listening!

KIT 17:

CLASS MEETUP SCHEDULING TEMPLATE

Time	Activity	Details
	Student introductions	
	Cultural activity 1	
	Cultural activity 2	
	Question Period	
	Goodbyes	

KIT 18:
FIELD JOURNAL FIRST ENTRY

Field Journal Entry #1

Researcher:
Subject of my observation:
Reasons why my field research benefits the community and the world:

I wonder …

1.
2.
3.
4.
5.

Current Photo/Illustration
Date: _____ Time: _____ Location: _____

KIT 19:

OBSERVATION LOG ENTRY

Observation Log

Subject: _____

Entry #: _____ Date: _____ Time: _____ Location: _____

Data Collected:

Photo/Drawing:	Notes:

KIT 20:

FIELD JOURNAL LAST ENTRY: FINDINGS AND CONCLUSIONS

Subject:

I began my field research wondering:

1.

2.

3.

4.

5.

At the end of my field research, I gathered these insights:

KIT 21:

TABLE OF ACHIEVEMENTS RECEIVED

Download available at ShellyTerrell.com/EdTechMissions

Achievement	Emblem (Draw it)	Awarded by...

KIT 22:

COMPLETED BADGE TABLE EXAMPLE

Digital Badge (image)	How do you earn this badge?	Example
Badge Name: EduStar Helper Website: Cred.ly	A teacher or peer issues this badge to a student who helped a peer with a learning task. The student did not complete the task or tell the peer the answers. Instead, the peer listened, demonstrated, and guided.	I saw Arthur show Suzie how to draw a monster. She kept erasing her monster and looked frustrated. Arthur said nice words then helped her try again. He then gave her verbal instructions which she followed. Her monster was cool!

KIT 23:
BADGE DESIGN TEMPLATE

Badge name:

Instructions: In the box below draw your badge.

Criteria (How do people earn the badge?):

Skills and achievements recognized:

Evidence (Describe the required evidence earners need to submit):

KIT 24:
COMPLETED BADGE FORM EXAMPLE

Earn The Gem Comment Badge Submission Form

CRITERIA

The earner demonstrates great skill in posting a comment. The comment is at least 2 or more sentences long and does at least one of the following: asks a thoughtful question, provides a relevant example, or summarizes and links to more research. The comment continues the conversation. The comment is also respectful and critiques or questions the ideas presented and does not attack the author. The comment is free of grammar and spelling errors.

First and Last Name:

_____

EVIDENCE

Copy and paste your comment below. Also, provide a link to your comment and the blog post.

Comment URL (Include http://):

_____

Comment (Copy/paste from blog):

_____

KIT 25:
CROWDFUND CAMPAIGN INQUIRY QUESTIONS

1. What is the title of the campaign?

2. What need does the campaign address?

3. What is the subject and age group?

4. What is the goal amount?

5. What do donations help fund?

6. What is the story behind the fundraising campaign?

7. Is it a convincing, compelling, and motivating story? Why?

8. Are there any images or videos associated with the campaign?

9. Is the campaign supported by any social media?

10. What do you like most about this campaign?

11. What one area would you improve to make this campaign more successful?

KIT 26:

MISSION CARDS

Print these mission cards to introduce students to each mission. Complete missions in any order you choose.

MISSION:
Design a game walkthrough

To accomplish this mission successfully your peers will need to complete a task in a game using a video walkthrough created by you.

OVERVIEW:

★ Choose a task in a game for your walkthrough

★ Provide clear and simple instructions

★ Design your walkthrough with a screencasting tool

 **HackLearning.org** *Await further details and resources.*
#EdTechMissions

MISSION:
Go on a selfie adventure

To accomplish this mission successfully you will complete several selfie challenges.

OVERVIEW:

★ Review the selfie challenges provided by your teacher

★ Take selfies to meet these challenges

★ Present your selfie adventure to your peers

 HackLearning.org *Await further details and resources.*
#EdTechMissions

MISSION:
Create a fictional social media profile

To accomplish this mission successfully you will manage the social media profile for a historical figure.

OVERVIEW:

★ Get to know your figure's personality and life

★ Create their social media profile

★ Post and interact with others as they might have

HACK
Learning
S E R I E S

HackLearning.org
#EdTechMissions

Await further details and resources.

MISSION:
Remix learning into a digital textbook

To accomplish this mission successfully you will design engaging learning content to include in our digital textbook.

OVERVIEW:

★ Use a web tool to layout learning materials

★ Attribute content created by others

★ Fuse text, animation, visuals, and audio

HACK
Learning
S E R I E S

HackLearning.org
#EdTechMissions

Await further details and resources.

MISSION:
Debate issues, don't diss people

To accomplish this mission successfully you will present a strong argument and respectfully counter-argue.

OVERVIEW:

★ Craft a strong claim with logical support

★ Respectfully debate issues following guidelines

★ Strategize to defeat the troll

HackLearning.org
#EdTechMissions

Await further details and resources.

MISSION:
Seek and preserve the truth

To accomplish this mission successfully you will collaborate with a news crew to produce a broadcast.

OVERVIEW:

★ Research your news topic

★ Write a script covering important points

★ Produce a newscast

HackLearning.org
#EdTechMissions

Await further details and resources.

MISSION:
Assemble a global class meetup

To accomplish this mission successfully you will video conference with a partner school to explore a pressing world issue.

OVERVIEW:

★ Video conference to exchange cultural knowledge

★ Teach the global partner about your country's experiences with a world issue

 HackLearning.org
#EdTechMissions
Await further details and resources.

MISSION:
Enlighten the world as a citizen scientist

To accomplish this mission successfully you will keep a field journal and publish your findings.

OVERVIEW:

★ Record your investigations in observation logs

★ Publish key findings

★ Share your key findings with an audience

 HackLearning.org
#EdTechMissions
Await further details and resources.

MISSION:
Appreciate others with a digital badge

To accomplish this mission successfully you will design a digital badge for peers to earn.

OVERVIEW:

★ Outline the criteria and evidence needed to earn the badge

★ Design and issue the digital badge

HACK
Learning
SERIES

HackLearning.org
#EdTechMissions

Await further details and resources.

MISSION:
Crowdfund innovation to find solutions

To complete this mission successfully you will collaborate with peers to crowdfund money for a need.

OVERVIEW:

★ Identify a need and do background research

★ Use a crowdfunding website to raise money to address the need

HACK
Learning
SERIES

HackLearning.org
#EdTechMissions

Await further details and resources.

KIT 27:
DIGITAL BADGES

Instructions: Print these digital badges to give to students for completing each mission. Download each digital badge as a PNG at ShellyTerrell.com/EdTechMissions.

DIGITAL DESIGNER CYBER MISSION

Mission 1: Design a Game Walkthrough

DIGITAL ADVENTURER CYBER MISSION

Mission 2: Go on a Selfie Adventure

SOCIAL MEDIA MANAGER CYBER MISSION

Mission 3: Create a Fictional Social Media Profile

DIGITAL AUTHOR CYBER MISSION

Mission 4: Remix Learning Into a Digital Textbook

DEBATE STAR
CYBER MISSION

Mission 5: Debate Issues, Don't Diss People

CITIZEN REPORTER
CYBER MISSION

Mission 6: Seek and Preserve the Truth

GLOBAL CITIZEN
CYBER MISSION

Mission 7: Assemble a Global Class Meetup

CITIZEN SCIENTIST
CYBER MISSION

Mission 8: Enlighten the World as a Citizen Scientist

BADGE DESIGNER
CYBER MISSION

Mission 9: Appreciate Others with a Digital Badge

CROWDFUNDER
CYBER MISSION

Mission 10: Crowdfund Innovation to Find Solutions

OTHER BOOKS IN THE
HACK LEARNING SERIES

HACKING EDUCATION
10 Quick Fixes For Every School

By Mark Barnes (@markbarnes19) & Jennifer Gonzalez (@cultofpedagogy)

In the bestselling *Hacking Education*, Mark Barnes and Jennifer Gonzalez employ decades of teaching experience and hundreds of discussions with education thought leaders to show you how to find and hone the quick fixes that every school and classroom need. Using a Hacker's mentality, they provide **one Aha moment after another** with 10 Quick Fixes For Every School – solutions to everyday problems and teaching methods that any teacher or administrator can implement immediately.

"Barnes and Gonzalez don't just solve problems; they turn teachers into hackers – a transformation that is right on time."
— DON WETTRICK, AUTHOR OF *PURE GENIUS*

MAKE WRITING
5 Teaching Strategies That Turn
Writer's Workshop Into a Maker Space

By Angela Stockman (@angelastockman)

Everyone's favorite education blogger and writing coach, Angela Stockman, turns teaching strategies and practices upside down in the bestselling, *Make Writing*. She spills you out of your chair, shreds your lined paper, and launches you and your writer's workshop into the maker space! Stockman provides five right-now writing strategies that reinvent instruction and **inspire both young and adult writers** to express ideas with tools that have rarely, if ever, been considered. *Make Writing* is a fast-paced journey inside Stockman's Western New York Young Writer's Studio, alongside the students there who learn how to write and how to make, employing Stockman's unique teaching methods.

"Offering suggestions for using new materials in old ways, thoughtful questions, and specific tips for tinkering and finding new audiences, this refreshing book is inspiring and practical in equal measure."

— AMY LUDWIG VANDERWATER, AUTHOR AND TEACHER

HACKING ASSESSMENT

10 Ways to Go Gradeless in a Traditional Grades School

By Starr Sackstein (@mssackstein)

In the bestselling *Hacking Assessment,* award-winning teacher and world-renowned formative assessment expert Starr Sackstein unravels one of education's oldest mysteries: How to assess learning without grades – even in a school that uses numbers, letters, GPAs, and report cards. While many educators can only muse about the possibility of a world without grades, teachers like Sackstein are **reimagining education**. In this unique, eagerly anticipated book, Sackstein shows you exactly how to create a remarkable no-grades classroom like hers, a vibrant place where students grow, share, thrive, and become independent learners who never ask, "What's this worth?"

"The beauty of the book is that it is not an empty argument against grades—but rather filled with valuable alternatives that are practical and will help to refocus the classroom on what matters most."

— ADAM BELLOW, WHITE HOUSE PRESIDENTIAL INNOVATION FELLOW

HACKING THE COMMON CORE
10 Strategies for Amazing Learning in a Standardized World

By Michael Fisher (@fisher1000)

In *Hacking the Common Core,* longtime teacher and CCSS specialist Mike Fisher shows you how to bring fun back to learning, with 10 amazing hacks for teaching all Core subjects, while engaging students and making learning fun. Fisher's experience and insights help teachers and parents better understand close reading, balancing fiction and nonfiction, using projects with the Core, and much more. *Hacking the Common Core* provides **read-tonight-implement-tomorrow strategies** for teaching the standards in fun and engaging ways, improving teaching and learning for students, parents, and educators.

HACKING LEADERSHIP
10 Ways Great Leaders Inspire Learning That Teachers, Students, and Parents Love

By Joe Sanfelippo (@joesanfelippoFC) and Tony Sinanis (@tonysinanis)

In the runaway bestseller *Hacking Leadership,* renowned school leaders Joe Sanfelippo and Tony Sinanis bring readers inside schools that few stakeholders have ever seen – places where students not only come first but have a unique voice in teaching and learning. Sanfelippo and Sinanis ignore the bureaucracy that stifles many leaders, focusing instead on building a culture of **engagement, transparency, and most important, fun.** *Hacking Leadership* has superintendents, principals, and teacher leaders around the world employing strategies they never before believed possible.

"The authors do a beautiful job of helping leaders focus inward, instead of outward. This is an essential read for leaders who are, or want to lead, learner-centered schools."

— **GEORGE COUROS,** AUTHOR OF *THE INNOVATOR'S MINDSET*

HACKING LITERACY
5 Ways To Turn Any Classroom Into a Culture Of Readers

By Gerard Dawson (@gerarddawson3)

In *Hacking Literacy*, classroom teacher, author, and reading consultant Gerard Dawson reveals 5 simple ways any educator or parent can turn even the most reluctant reader into a thriving, enthusiastic lover of books. Dawson cuts through outdated pedagogy and standardization, turning reading theory into practice, sharing **valuable reading strategies**, and providing what *Hack Learning Series* readers have come to expect – actionable, do-it-tomorrow strategies that can be built into long-term solutions.

HACKING ENGAGEMENT
50 Tips & Tools to Engage Teachers and Learners Daily

By James Alan Sturtevant (@jamessturtevant)

Some students hate your class. Others are just bored. Many are too nice, or too afraid, to say anything about it. Don't let it bother you; it happens to the best of us. But now, it's **time to engage!** In *Hacking Engagement*, the seventh book in the *Hack Learning Series*, veteran high school teacher, author, and popular podcaster James Sturtevant provides 50 – that's right five-oh – tips and tools that will engage even the most reluctant learners daily.

HACKING HOMEWORK
10 Strategies That Inspire Learning Outside the Classroom

By Starr Sackstein (@mssackstein) and Connie Hamilton (@conniehamilton)

Learning outside the classroom is being reimagined, and student engagement is better than ever. World-renowned author/educator Starr Sackstein has changed how teachers around the world look at traditional grades. Now she's teaming with veteran educator, curriculum director, and national presenter Connie Hamilton to bring you **10 powerful strategies** for teachers and parents that promise to inspire independent learning at home, without punishments or low grades.

"Starr Sackstein and Connie Hamilton have assembled a book full of great answers to the question, 'How can we make homework engaging and meaningful?'"

— DOUG FISHER AND NANCY FREY, AUTHORS AND PRESENTERS

HACKING PROJECT BASED LEARNING
10 Easy Steps to PBL and Inquiry in the Classroom

By Ross Cooper (@rosscoops31) and Erin Murphy (@murphysmusings5)

As questions and mysteries around PBL and inquiry continue to swirl, experienced classroom teachers and school administrators Ross Cooper and Erin Murphy have written a book that will empower those intimidated by PBL to cry, "I can do this!" while at the same time providing added value for those who are already familiar with the process. *Hacking Project Based Learning* demystifies what

PBL is all about with **10 hacks that construct a simple path** that educators and students can easily follow to achieve success.

"*Hacking Project Based Learning* is a classroom essential. Its ten simple 'hacks' will guide you through the process of setting up a learning environment in which students will thrive from start to finish."
— **DANIEL H. PINK**, *NEW YORK TIMES* BESTSELLING AUTHOR OF *DRIVE*

HACK LEARNING ANTHOLOGY
Innovative Solutions for Teachers and Leaders

Edited by Mark Barnes (@markbarnes19)

Anthology brings you the most innovative education Hacks from the first nine books in the *Hack Learning Series*. Written by twelve award-winning classroom teachers, principals, superintendents, college instructors, and international presenters, *Anthology* is every educator's new problem-solving handbook. It is both a preview of nine other books and a **full-fledged, feature-length blueprint** for solving your biggest school and classroom problems.

HACKING GOOGLE FOR EDUCATION
99 Ways to Leverage Google Tools in Classrooms, Schools, and Districts

By Brad Currie (@bradmcurrie), Billy Krakower (@wkrakower), and Scott Rocco (@ScottRRocco)

If you could do more with Google than search, what would it be? Would you use Google Hangouts to connect students to cultures around the world? Would you finally achieve a paperless workflow with Classroom? Would you inform and engage stakeholders district-wide through Blogger? Now, you can say "Yes" to all of these, because Currie, Krakower, and Rocco remove the limits in

Hacking Google for Education, giving you **99 Hacks in 33 chapters**, covering Google in a unique way that benefits all stakeholders.

"Connected educators have long sought a comprehensive resource for implementing blended learning with G Suite. *Hacking Google for Education* superbly delivers with a plethora of classroom-ready solutions and linked exemplars."
— DR. ROBERT R. ZYWICKI, SUPERINTENDENT OF WEEHAWKEN TOWNSHIP SCHOOL DISTRICT

HACKING ENGAGEMENT AGAIN
50 Teacher Tools That Will Make Students Love Your Class

By James Alan Sturtevant (@jamessturtevant)

50 Student Engagement Hacks just weren't enough. 33-year veteran classroom teacher, James Alan Sturtevant, wowed teachers with the original *Hacking Engagement*, which contained 50 Tips and Tools to Engage Teachers and Learners Daily. Those educators and students got better, but they craved more. So, longtime educator and wildly popular student engager Sturtevant is *Hacking Engagement Again*!

HACK LEARNING RESOURCES

All Things Hack Learning:

hacklearning.org

The Entire *Hack Learning Series* on Amazon:

hacklearningbooks.com

The Hack Learning Podcast, hosted by Mark Barnes:

hacklearningpodcast.com

Hack Learning on Twitter:

@HackMyLearning

#HackLearning

#HackingLeadership

#HackingLiteracy

#HackingEngagement

#HackingHomework

#HackingPBL

#MakeWriting

#HackGoogleEdu

#EdTechMissions

#ParentMantras

#MovieTeacher

Hack Learning on Facebook:

facebook.com/hacklearningseries

Hack Learning on Instagram:

hackmylearning

The Hack Learning Academy:

hacklearningacademy.com

MEET THE AUTHOR

Shelly Sanchez Terrell is an international speaker, eLearning specialist, professor, and the author of *The 30 Goals Challenge for Teachers*. She has trained teachers and taught language learners in more than twenty countries as an invited guest expert by organizations like UNESCO Bangkok, Cultura Inglesa of Brazil, the British Council in Tel Aviv, and the U.S. Embassy in Venezuela. Shelly is the 2015 National Association of Professional Women's Woman of the Year. Several notable entities, such as The New York Times, NPR, and Microsoft's Heroes for Education, recognize her as an innovator in the movement of teacher-driven professional development. She holds a Bammy Award as a founder of #Edchat. Her latest project is the creation of Edspeakers to enrich the field of education with passionate, diverse voices. Shelly's greatest joy is being the proud mother of Savannah Duncan-Sanchez and Rosco the pug.

She has an Honors BA in English with a minor in Communication and a specialization in Electronic Media from UTSA, a master's degree in Curriculum Instruction from the University of Phoenix, and a CELTA from CELT Athens. She regularly shares her tips for effective technology integration via TeacherRebootCamp.com and Twitter (@ShellTerrell).

ACKNOWLEDGEMENTS

WRITING A BOOK takes the support and help of many people. Authors need to surround themselves with champions who believe in them, inspire them, and constantly motivate them. Since 2013, I've blogged about sending students on learning missions. I've had the idea for this book for a long time and it took meeting the right publisher to make it come to fruition. Thank you to Mark Barnes who encouraged me to publish these digital learning missions and put a framework to my ideas. I'm grateful for his guidance and for connecting me to the amazing project manager, Rebecca Morris. Rebecca was there throughout the process to make sure the content shined. I will miss working with her.

I dedicate this book foremost to my beautiful daughter, Savannah Simone Duncan-Sanchez. I never thought I could write a book with a newborn, but she was there to make sure I took the time to play and enjoy life. On each break, I gained ideas for each mission. I wrote each mission with my daughter in mind. I wanted to inspire and provide practical tips for her future teachers to send her on digital learning missions.

One day Savannah will make an impact on the world, guided by great educators like the ones who shared their teaching anecdotes. Thank you to André Spang, Anthippi Harou, Jon Samuelson, Colleen Rose, Noah Geisel, Andrea Santilli, and Kelly Jake Duncan who brought each mission to life. Thanks also to Marijana Smolcec and her son Filip Smolcec for showing me how children are already doing great things on the internet. I appreciate all the students I've taught who have completed missions in ways I never could have imagined.

A special thanks to my partner, Kelly Jake Duncan, who exemplifies what great teachers do in the classroom. He is also an amazing father who offered support and took care of baby Savannah while mommy finished her book. I was also blessed to have Rosco the pug by my side as he has been with every book!

PUBLICATIONS

Times 10 is helping all education stakeholders improve every aspect of teaching and learning. We are committed to solving big problems with simple ideas. We bring you content from experts, shared through multiple channels, including books, podcasts, and an array of social networks. Our mantra is simple: Read it today; fix it tomorrow. Stay in touch with us at HackLearning. org, at #HackLearning on Twitter, and on the Hack Learning Facebook group.

CPSIA information can be obtained
at www.ICGtesting.com
Printed in the USA
LVHW02*1655220718
584575LV00010B/143/P